FREEDOM OF THE PRESSES

ARTISTS' BOOKS IN THE TWENTY-FIRST CENTURY

FREEDOM OF THE PRESSES

Freedom of the Presses

Artists' Books in the Twenty-first Century

Edited by Marshall Weber
Book design by Will Brady
Cover design by Marshall Weber and Will Brady
Endpapers by Josh MacPhee
Proofreading by Tracey Ober, Sarah Ream, Paula Solimano
Spanish/English translation by Tracey Ober and Paula Solimano

Special thanks to Joshua Kurtz, Aimee Lusty, Maya Taylor, and Felice Tebbe. Thanks to all the activists, archivists, artists, curators, collectors, fans, librarians, patrons, readers, sponsors, teachers, writers, and Booklyn's board and staff for making this book possible.

Published by Booklyn, Brooklyn, NY

ISBN 978-0-692-16678-9

For more information about Booklyn visit booklyn.org
For textbook orders write: Marshall Weber at mweber@booklyn.org

This publication is made possible in part by the New York State Council on the Arts with the support of Governor Andrew M. Cuomo and the New York State Legislature.

Contents

Dedicated to Chicano activist, artist, and curator René Yañez, 1942–2018.
His teachings provided the seed for this book.

FREEDOM OF THE PRESSES

ALL
ABOUT
HOUSE
PLANTS

KURT ALLERSLEV

A Closed Book is a Treasure Trove of Wild Possibility

WHAT HAPPENS IN A BOOK when you're not reading it? A closed book is a treasure trove of wild possibility. The insides of a book when it sits closed on the shelf are not like the light in the refrigerator when you close the door—you know that light goes out every time. It's designed to do that. Even if you don't see the light go out, you know it has.

The bookmaker, however, creates something that is meant to endure. The insides—text and/or images—stay lit up forever. But perhaps they wonder if you have gone out. They don't know about the continuance of our existence when the book is closed. What do we become to the closed book? What do the pollution, the cat, the car alarms and moldy ham sandwiches matter to a closed book? In closing, the book protects itself from the chaos that seeks to diminish and extinguish the beauty within.

Left: *All About Houseplants*, 2000, Kurt Allerslev and Mark Wagner, unique artists' book. Photo: Kurt Allerslev

Right: *Self-portrait in egg shell*, 2004, Kurt Allerslev. Photo: the artist

I don't believe that the insides of closed books have secret lives in the way that we have a secret life when we close our eyes and dream. We are able to escape our everyday reality, exchange it for fleeting moments of other. The book, however, is also not statically waiting for us to indulge it—rather it grows and matures with each passing moment. The outside world creates a new patina. The pages yellow, the text grows more meaningful and wise, or more dated and doddering. As the world changes, as wars are fought, babies born, and species go extinct, the context is altered. A book is fed by every pair of eyes that fall on it; in turn, the insides of that book pay homage to the creators—the authors, the artists who make it—by providing the reader with a passage to a secret life that can only be accessed by opening it—as if dreaming.

You can't open the same book twice. Perhaps you can't even open the same book once. Like a river, it's changing as you open it. As the pages turn. And it changes as it sits on the shelf. A library full of books is a whirlpool of persistent change. We want text to solidify language, but language is too fluid. We are too fluid.

TIA BLASSINGAME

Dear Book Arts

African American Artists and the Book Form

IF YOU ARE AN EDUCATOR, librarian, artist, scholar, collector, curator, I am going to tell you things that you should already know and should be implementing. If you are a student, hopefully this will help you start experimenting with the book form in your own budding art practice and as a method of exploring your identity, culture, and history.

There are plenty of African American artists working in the book form. There should be more, but their movement into the field needs to be nurtured so they will remain and flourish. If they are not welcome, they will immediately retreat. Their presence in and introduction to the book arts

What's Happening With Momma, 1988, Clarissa Sligh, editioned artists' book. Photo: the artist

field should be welcomed and encouraged. They may very well be the future of this art form.

STUDENTS

Yes, it is okay to make books about your identity and culture. This world might just need it. If your instructors and professors don't support you, look to other mentors—artists, art historians, religious and community leaders, community organizers, and activists. Study African American artists, printers, printmakers—those working in the book form and those who do not. Familiarize yourself with their work. Ask librarians, faculty, artists, scholars about the *Coast to Coast: Women Artists of Color Artists' Books Project* exhibition, organized by Faith Ringgold with the aid of Clarissa Sligh and Margaret Gallegos, that featured two hundred artists of color representing over thirty states and toured nationally in the late 1980s and early 1990s. Check the websites of booksellers like Booklyn and Vamp & Tramp and organizations like Women's Studio Workshop and National Museum of Women in the Arts for other African American artists working in the book form. Look at the print and book work of majority artists like Maureen Cummins, Ann Tyler, Alan Governor, and Fred Hagstrom that features African American history and culture. Are their lens and focus different from that of African American artists? What can you learn from their treatments? Are the treatments genuine, exploitive, enlightening? Learn to look with a critical eye at all work about your history and identity regardless of authorship.

Here is a list of artists' books by African American artists to get you started:

- *Edges* by Alisa Banks (2009)
- *Rosenwald* by Alisa Banks (2013)
- *Anniversary* by Tia Blassingame (2011)
- *Harvest: holding & trading* by Tia Blassingame (2013)
- *Reparations* by Emory Douglas (2010)
- *Strange Fruit: Words Protesting Lynchings and Burnings* by Amos Kennedy, Jr. (1994)
- *Transforming Hate* by Clarissa Sligh (2016)
- *What's Happening With Momma?* by Clarissa Sligh (1988)
- *America, Guests Who Came to Dinner (and Stayed)* by Evelyn Patricia Terry (2016)
- *Freedom, a Fable* by Kara Walker (1997)

Ruth Ellis, 1940. Photographer unknown.

- *In the event anyone disappears* by Bisa Washington (1991)
- *Promise not to tell* by Bisa Washington (2007)

EDUCATORS/PRACTITIONERS

Be aware of your prejudices and how they may be affecting your critique of book and print work by students of color. If your students' artists' books feature content about race and ethnicity of which you are ignorant and which makes you uncomfortable, acknowledge this and look for ways to provide constructive feedback nonetheless. If that is simply beyond you at the moment, do some research. Talk to your colleagues in the Africana or African American Studies or Art History departments. Find an expert or scholar who can help you educate yourself and who may be willing to give students feedback on content, when, in the

Tuskegee Institute printing class, 1902. Photographer unknown.

early stages of your education, you are limited to giving feedback on formal elements. Whether your students' focus is color theory or cultural identity, whether it is inspired by their own history and culture or by a known-to-you white artist, you are expected to—much like an attorney—educate yourself enough to support your students regardless of their sex, race, identity, background. Every student deserves thoughtful and thorough critique on formal elements *and* content. Lastly, do not take on only interns and protégés that look like you. Provide mentorship and internship opportunities to African Americans interested in the field. Offer an internship with a stipend; crowdfund it, if necessary.

SCHOLARS

Write us in. Submit your research and papers on African American printers and printmakers, bookbinders, and artists working in the book form to book arts, printmaking, and book/print-history conferences, journals, and websites. When you organize conferences and symposiums on African American book and print history, post the information to book arts listservs and online forums. Let book arts and printmaking departments and certificate programs know; their students might be very interested.

Many African American college and graduate students are creating prints and artists' books about race and ethnicity. Through isolation and a lack of knowledge, they feel like solitary pioneers without known histories or examples of African American artists and printers to inspire them. Without exposure to the likes of Dox Thrash, Elizabeth Catlett, Alison Saar, Ruth Ellis, and so many pioneers of print, they lack significant history and inspiration. They miss the insight to see quilts by the many forgotten African Americans or those by the celebrated Gee's Bend quilters or by Faith Ringgold as artworks with arguably strong bookish characteristics. You might be surprised by the ignorance of their professors on these topics.

LIBRARIANS

More often than not, you and your collections introduce artists' books, fine press books and the very notion of book arts to audiences young and old. Take your time; read the books in your collection. If the artist is still living,

Anniversary, 2011, Tia Blassingame, editioned artists' book.
Photo: the artist

Hades DWP, 2017, Alison Saar and Samiya Bashir, editioned artists' book.
Photo: Courtesy of LA Louver Gallery

reach out and ask questions. In your collection development efforts, look for artists' books by diverse voices that will help your student, faculty, and public patrons make sense of current events and challenging topics such as institutional racism, voting rights, socio-economic inequalities.

To college and university librarians, particularly those at Art and Design schools, offer an annual book arts prize that includes purchase prizes and an exhibition of entries. Give the winning artists a forum to present and sell their work. Consider commissioning limited-edition work from the winner, if their portfolio seems particularly promising and they are interested. Reach out to student organizations, especially those for marginalized students; invite their membership to participate. Reduce and waive any entry fees. Don't just be dazzled by visuals: read the content. Maybe there is a piece that has significant content but whose formal elements or craft are rudimentary. In acknowledgement of the richness of content and ideas, offer such entries a runner-up prize or give the entrant the opportunity to learn basics from a local bindery or printshop. Above all, be creative and inclusive in your approach.

Our turbulent times roiling with newly uncloaked racism, with anti-Semitic, anti-Muslim, anti-LGBTQ, and misogynistic hate-filled rhetoric should motivate you to make and keep your book arts collection as a relevant refuge and incubator of ideas for your users, particularly your younger patrons as they expand their comprehension of and begin

to speak from a place of knowledge about the world, with its marvels and horrors.

PROFESSIONAL ORGANIZATIONS

I recently spoke with a representative of the local chapter of a national book arts organization about the group's desire to appeal to younger members and diversify the group. By her own admision, the membership at that time consisted overwhelmingly of older white women. During the conversation, she focused completely on the problem of attracting younger members. At the end of our discussion, I asked her about diversity. In response, she asked me if I could suggest any local African American organizations or artists that the group might contact. I was shocked and disappointed. So I will say here what I was too upset to say to her and her group without off-color remarks.

Do not ask people of color for a binder of black folks, of brown folks, or any other folks. Do the work. Do the research. Educate yourself about African American artists and printers that use the book form and those who do not. Talk to curators. Visit collections and museums with a focus on African American art and culture. Go to community art centers, public schools and libraries in communities that are not your own. Get out of your comfort zone. Partner with HBCUs (Historically Black Colleges) and non-profits, black professional organizations. Consider lowering or waiving membership fees to attract members who may otherwise not be able to afford them. Are you representative of our diverse country or are your

Mami (or, how to know a goddess when you see one), 2016, Alison Saar and Evie Shockley, editioned artists' book. Photo: John Wynn

meetings filled with members who are overwhelmingly white? Are you inviting and promoting only members who look like you or are younger versions of yourselves? When African American members or interested parties like students attend your functions, conferences, or workshops are they met with stares and silence, or do your established members actively welcome them and introduce them to other members? Statement of the obvious: if they are there, at the very least, they are curious about book arts. If they have paid membership fees, they are interested. If they paid membership and conference fees, airfare, and for hotel rooms, they are committed to the field and in love with its power and possibility. They can see lucidly how it compliments their practice. Remember that feeling?

When their introduction to the profession is silence and stares, you announce with trumpets that you do not want them there and they are not welcome. Many will not return to your group; many will leave the field. Their absence affects generations of future African American practitioners, educators, curators, librarians, book/print scholars and, most of all, students. The direct effect upon your associations and organizations is that they are rendered irrelevant to an increasingly diverse population. In some cases, the problem is so extreme that your membership will soon be on the verge of extinction due to willful maintenance of a largely white membership and leadership as well as an inability or reluctance to diversify. If your group belongs to a city or region whose population is ethnically and racially diverse but does not reflect that:

1. Shame on you for not adequately representing your locale.
2. Get to it. Use the percentages in your region or city as your minimum targets for representation in your membership and leadership.
3. If you have zero to negligible representation of African Americans in your leadership positions, again shame on you.
4. Consider offering conference scholarships that include conference fees and cover travel expenses.

COLLECTORS

To private collectors and public collections of artifacts, manuscripts, paintings, and sculptures by African American artists and craftspeople of cultural significance, consider adding artists' books and prints to your collections. These pieces with which, with care, you might physically interact could very well synthesize and connect the histories and artifacts that you collect in ways you have never imagined. I challenge you to support and give access to African American artists working in the book form. Their work may provide a different but more approachable way for the public to understand and access your collections.

CONCLUSION

For many selfish reasons, I want to see increased representation in this field that I love. I want it to more fully represent our nation, particularly as it browns. More distinctive and diverse voices working in the book form will keep the field vibrant and relevant as the nation's demographics shift.

The book arts field has a long way to go, but maybe the current climate since the 2017 election, a climate that has energized hate groups and racist, misogynist, anti-semitic, anti-Muslim, anti-disabled, anti-LGBTQ, and anti-transgender bullying acts and rhetoric can ignite all those in the field to give a hand up to artists and students of color who might contribute their stories and voices to the book form. Without increased African American participation, how will the books arts field remain relevant? How will it provide thoughtful counterpoint to hate speech and ignorance? How will it provide a way for people of different beliefs and backgrounds to talk about and understand race and racism? It won't.

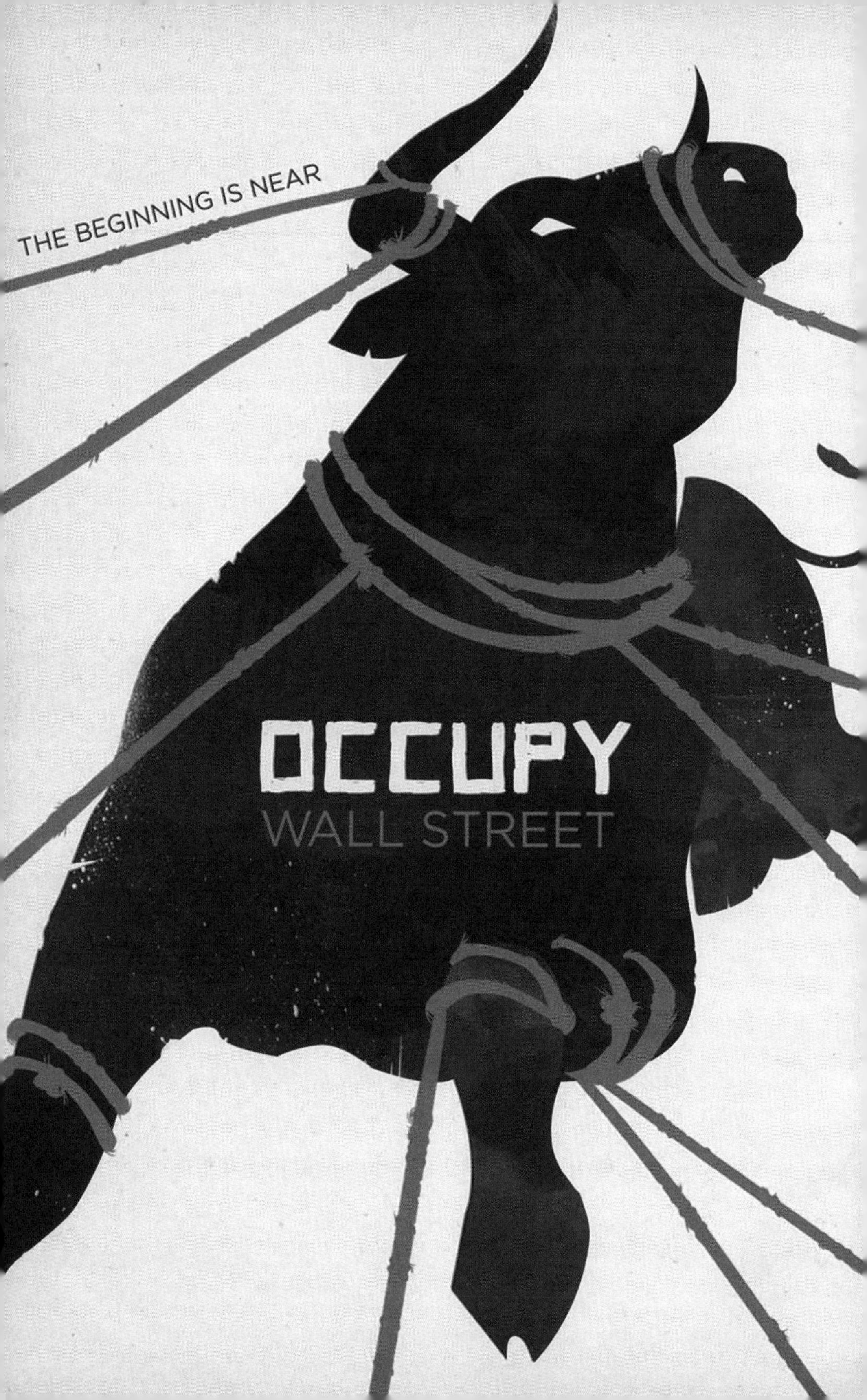

THE BEGINNING IS NEAR

OCCUPY

WALL STREET

SARAH KIRK HANLEY

A Place for Activist Art
Booklyn and Twenty-first-century Agitprop

IN A RECENT STATEMENT published by Booklyn, the Egyptian activist artist Ganzeer delineates a distinction between "art that delivers commentary from a safe distance" and that which is "participatory . . . [and deals] with the immediate struggles and concerns of the audience."[1] The artist aligns himself with the latter, and his work is a breathing example of this subcategory of political art that has been called many names, from "activist art" to "radical art" to "agitprop" to "street art." As noted by Nicolas Lampert in his exceptional survey of activist art in the U.S., "Many people look to the world of museums and galleries when they think of visual art . . . [but] these places are not the primary site for *activist art*."[2] Where, then, can it be found? By its very nature, activist art takes place on the ground and in the moment. Accounts and records tend to be piecemeal and firsthand.

With a few notable exceptions, the history is rarely formalized into a cohesive narrative, as art histories often overlook such grassroots work in favor of passive forms of political commentary by mainstream artists.[3] However, in recent years, Booklyn—a non-profit collective that serves artists working in book or portfolio formats—has stepped in to fill an essential role in centralizing and promoting activist art, providing vital resources and means of distribution.[4]

The Beginning is Near, 2012, Alexandra Clotfelter, offset lithograph (included in the 20 copies of Occuprint portfolio pre-publication sponsor's edition). Photo: Booklyn

Ganzeer is one of many activist artists and organizations currently represented by Booklyn, which was founded in 1999 by Kurt Allerslev, Sara Parkel, Peter Spagnuolo, Mark Wagner, Marshall Weber, and Christopher Wilde to promote contemporary artists' books and publications. Then, as today, Booklyn's purview is global and multifarious, but street art has always been an important aspect of its ethos. Weber explains, "In general the culture was punk, radical, and collectivist . . . at the beginning the focus was more overtly in the material nature of artists' books as 'art' but the inclination to political activism was apparent . . . even at that time."[5] This tendency catalyzed to a deeper commitment following the events of September 11, 2001 and subsequent Homeland Security policies enacted by the Bush Administration. In response to the tragedies of that day, Booklyn published two collaborative publications: *Eleven* (book & CD, editions of 29 and 19, 2002), and distributed Sara Parkel's Filter Press's *...Even the Birds Were on Fire...For the Victims of Violence* (letterpress, edition of 150, 2001). Both books were designed to crystallize and memorialize events; they included photographs, first-hand accounts, poetry, and essays. Booklyn also organized a touring exhibition of these publications and related unique works with the aim of fomenting anti-war sentiment.

Relationships established early on with Xu Bing and artists in the squatter movement in the Lower East Side of Manhattan established a foundation for activist art that has now grown to dominate Booklyn's program. Xu, who is arguably its most renowned artist-member, first began to work with Booklyn in 2004. His canonical *Book from the Sky* (1987–91), an installation of scrolls and accordion-folded books comprised of invented/nonsensical Chinese characters, significantly contributed to the cultural changes that attended the democracy movement in China. A physically impressive project that took years to complete, it has been interpreted as both a comment on the general limitations of language and knowledge and a specific jab at Maoist doctrine and government. The work was shown twice in Beijing during October 1988 and February 1989 and was denounced in official newspapers by the Ministry of Culture (which shut down the second exhibition in response to a performance piece by another artist). Within the movement, Xu's project was celebrated for its revolutionary subject matter and its artistic impact: it had accomplished a hitherto unattainable fusion of traditional Chinese culture and contemporary global art trends, and its impact is still being felt today. Later, Xu and fellow Chinese artists Ai Weiwei and Zeng Xiaojun self-published a trilogy of radical publications for underground distribution titled *The Black Cover Book* (1994), *The White Cover Book* (1995), and *The Gray Cover Book* (1997) in editions of 3,000. The books contained political texts as well as information about important twentieth-century Western artists and movements that were hitherto unknown to their colleagues in China and had a major impact on the now burgeoning contemporary art scene there.[6]

Booklyn has a long-term relationship with a number of artists involved with *World War 3 Illustrated*, a graphic-novel-style news and commentary magazine founded in 1979 in New York. The zine embraces radical politics and each semi-annual issue is dedicated to a theme. *The Riot Issue* (#11, 1989) covered the Tompkins Square Riot of 1988 and the anti-gentrification movement in the Lower East Side of Manhattan; many of the neighborhood's artists were losing their homes. *Your House is Mine*, a book represented by Booklyn and published by alternative art venue Bullet Space in 1990, was also a response to these events, intended to be "an implicit demonstration that art can function as a means of resistance."[7] The collection of prints, essays, timelines, and articles documents residents' struggles with affordable housing, the AIDS crisis, and big-money real-estate development (ironically, Donald Trump is specifically called out). In addition to a limited edition of 150, the publication was released and distributed in newspaper format and featured on the cover of *Artforum* in 1991. Fly-o, an activist squatter/homesteader who arrived in New York at that time, also contributed to this cause in thousands of zines and comix (such as *PEOPs*, *Dog Dayz*, and *Zero Content*), which were recently exhibited at Booklyn in a 2015 exhibition titled *Last Squat City: A Fly's Personal Archive*. She has been involved with Booklyn from its founding.

This type of material represented a relatively small segment of Booklyn's wares in the early aughts, but a culture shift toward agitprop began to take shape mid decade. Wagner and Wilde left to pursue other

War Is Trauma, 2011, Jesse Purcell, screenprint, from the *War Is Trauma* portfolio. Photo: the artist

Justseeds members Nicolas Lampert and Pete Railand wheatpasting posters from the *War Is Trauma* portfolio in the Rogers Park area of Chicago, November 15, 2010. Photo: Justseeds

interests, and Weber—an activist artist—took the helm as director, working with the board (chaired by Allerslev) and a core group of staff, including curator Felice Tebbe and managing director Maya Taylor, who joined in 2007 and 2011, respectively. He traveled extensively, and his interests in artists working outside of conventional norms led to important encounters with the organizers of other collective artist groups, particularly Justseeds Artists' Cooperative, which has since become a strong collaborator.

Weber describes Booklyn's revised focus as "a concentrated effort to shift the academic dialogue on artists' books away from materially-based, antiquarian, Anglo-centric aesthetics to content-based contemporary work by diverse international artists."[8] This new initiative played out through a vigorous campaign to place Booklyn artists' work into important public collections (museums and library special collections), an active traveling exhibition program, and heightened participation in art and book fairs globally. One of Booklyn's notable early accomplishments was to place the archive for Eric Drooker's award-winning graphic novel *FLOOD!* in the Library of Congress;[9] since then, the staff has successfully placed hundreds of limited-edition books, zines, portfolios, and archives in numerous public collections around the country and in Europe—most recently, placing the archive of René Yañez, artist and founder of Galería de la Raza in San Francisco, in the collection of the University of California, Berkeley.

The traveling exhibition program, which began in 2004 and averages two to three shows per year, exposes Booklyn artists and publications to a wide audience nationwide. Topics vary in scope and ambition, but among the most notable are *Found in Translation*, which first opened in 2006 at the San Francisco Center for the Book and continues to tour, and *Diamond Leaves: Artist Books from Around the World*, an exhibition co-curated by Xu and Weber that opened in 2012 at the Central Academy of Fine Arts in Beijing. The latter was the first major museum exhibition of contemporary artists' books in China and has now become a triennial.

Booklyn has also been a highly visible presence on the fair network over the past decade, exhibiting at Frankfurt Book Fair (2002–09), Editions/Artists' Book Fair (since 2004), NY Art Book Fair (since 2005), Art Libraries Society of North America Conference (2006–12), Codex Foundation Book Fair (since 2007, biannual), and LA Art Book Fair (since 2013), as well as other smaller fairs such as Manhattan Fine Press Book Fair and Comic Arts Brooklyn. Weber observes that, with the exception of Printed Matter's NYABF, "Booklyn has been seen to provide a more radical and diverse political perspective to these art and book fairs."[10]

In recent years, Booklyn's stake in activist art has intensified through numerous co-publishing projects with other collectives, especially Justseeds and Iraq Veterans Against the War (IVAW). [In 2016 IVAW renamed itself About Face: Veterans Against the War.] This relationship began to take shape in 2006 when Booklyn first represented the Combat Paper Project (CPP), a program in which veterans transform used uniforms into paper and artwork. CPP is headed by Drew Matott and Drew Cameron; their connection to Aaron Hughes, an activist artist, veteran, and organizer for IVAW, eventually led to a meeting between Weber and Hughes in 2007 at a book fair at Columbia College Chicago. Soon thereafter, Hughes began to work with Booklyn to publish chapbooks such as the *Warrior Writers* series (edited by Lovella Calica, 2008–12); *ABC #7: Not My Enemy* (2008), and Hughes' *Dust Memories* (2008). Meanwhile, Weber also met Justseeds founder Josh MacPhee through zine artist Erica Lyle (a.k.a. Iggy Scam). Justseeds self-describes as "a decentralized network of 30 artists committed to social, environmental, and political engagement."[11] Booklyn began to represent Justseeds publications shortly afterward; the first was *Resourced* (2010).

The first major co-publishing project between IVAW, Justseeds, and Booklyn began to take shape in 2010, when Hughes and Justseeds member Lampert co-organized *Operation Exposure: War Is Trauma*. The action was a series of events in Chicago surrounding Veterans Day that included rallies, readings, and public art displays.[12] Justseeds artists created posters and organized to wheatpaste them throughout the city along with an IVAW press release and stenciled portraits of affected soldiers.[13] The intention was to raise awareness of the devastating effects of redeployment on soldiers suffering from war-related psychosomatic trauma—including Post Traumatic Stress Disorder (PTSD), Traumatic Brain Injury (TBI), and Military Sexual Trauma (MST)—who are thereby denied the opportunity to heal from their injuries. Booklyn subsequently published the posters together

Celebrate People's History: Iraq Veterans Against the War—Ten Years of Fighting for Peace and Justice, 2012, various artists, editioned box set. Photo: Booklyn

in a limited-edition box set *War Is Trauma* (2011), thereby promoting and extending the message beyond the short life of these actions while also raising funds to cover expenses.[14] MacPhee comments, "Everything we do is self-funded and on an extremely thin budget . . . we had this idea that we could package and sell our work to self-fund and promote our ideas but had no idea how make that happen . . . Booklyn stepped in with a pre-existing distribution and funding network that has been essential to our projects."[15]

Shortly after the *War Is Trauma* set was published, the Occupy Movement erupted in Zuccotti Park. MacPhee and Jesse Goldstein were key organizers, and Justseeds member Kevin Caplicki helped to print a selection of posters from Occuprint, an affiliate of the Occupy movement that distributed agitprop posters. Occuprint arose from Issue 4 of the *Occupied Wall Street Journal* (OWSJ), which contained a selection of posters intended for public use; it was printed in an edition of 20,000 and distributed on the streets. The initial call for designs had received an overwhelming response but only a handful could be printed; the remainder were posted online for open access. Shortly thereafter, Goldstein and Weber hatched a plan to publish a selection of the posters in a limited box set to raise funds for the movement, modeled on the success of the *War Is Trauma* publication. Again, only a small portion of the hundreds submitted could be included; Goldstein explains that the selection was difficult and their curatorial process was governed by pre-established principles and a desire to represent the scope of submissions.[16] Booklyn co-published the box set, raising funds for the final edition of 100 with a Kickstarter campaign and through sales of deluxe pre-publication sponsorship box sets to select institutions and collectors. As with the Justseeds project, the Occupy movement was able to use the resulting funds from the publication of the box set to offset expenses and re-invest in its cause.[17]

The ten-year anniversary of IVAW in 2014 prompted a major new collaborative publication between Justseeds, Booklyn, and IVAW, titled *Celebrate People's History: Iraq Veterans Against the War—Ten Years of Fighting for Peace and Justice*. The portfolio "highlights key ideas, moments, projects, tactics, and individuals from IVAW history in order to uplift IVAW's ongoing struggle, inspire others to take action, and preserve the movement's history for future generations."[18] MacPhee says that it has been the most comprehensive collaboration to date between Booklyn and Justseeds (Hughes joined in 2013): "Booklyn was involved with the conceptualization from the start and raised the start-up funds by pre-selling deluxe portfolios."[19] Hughes spearheaded the project, organizing myriad artists and veteran contributors with the help of Siri Margerin from the Civilian-Soldier Alliance. Jesse Purcell, a Justseeds member and contributor to both IVAW portfolios, printed the new portfolio at his Repetitive Press imprint in Toronto.

MacPhee, Hughes, and Purcell agree that they learned a great deal from the earlier project and applied those lessons to the new publication.[20] The prospectus/tabloid tool kit took the form of an open-edition broadside that included a selection of full-size posters (similar to the OWSJ issue) and was distributed widely for the purpose of wheatpasting in public spaces (it includes step-by-step instructions for making the glue and adhering the posters to walls). Hughes also organized several wheatpasting and projection events of the posters in various cities, including Detroit, Chicago, and Oakland. The limited box set included the broadside, sixty-nine posters, a catalog of the works, and a reader with essays by members of IVAW, Justseeds, and others from Vietnam Veterans Against the War (edition of 116). The aforementioned deluxe sponsorship portfolios (edition of 20) included IVAW ephemera and memorabilia gathered by Hughes—such as Combat Paper projects, booklets, and flyers—as well as a unique drawing by the artist.

The Justseeds/Booklyn collaboration has continued to expand. In addition to its co-publication projects, Booklyn represents many of the cooperative's affiliate-member projects as well as projects co-published with other organizations, such as *Migration Now!* and *We Are the Storm* (co-published with CultureStrike, "a national pro-migrant" art collective in the Bay Area headed by Justseeds member Favianna Rodriguez). Justseeds projects are also featured in Booklyn-organized exhibitions like *Up Against the Wall* at the Brooklyn Art Gallery from August 30 to September 27, 2015, which featured selections from the *Celebrate People's History/IVAW* portfolio and *Imaging Apartheid*, a collection of posters in support of the Palestinian struggle for liberation. Booklyn and Justseeds members have also co-published a zine titled *Librarians and Archivists with Palestine* (2013) in support of the same movement.

In the past few years, Booklyn's program has expanded beyond U.S. borders to encompass a more global scope. Projects by the Mexican political-art collectives La Escuela de Cultura Popular Revolucionaria Mártires del 68 and Sublevarte Colectivo have transpired through connections to Justseeds members and Interference Archive in Brooklyn (a side project founded in part by three Justseeds members: MacPhee, Caplicki, and Molly Fair), which serves as an open-access archive of activist movements worldwide. Booklyn's international purview further expanded with the publication of a box set of the work of squatter-activist Keg de Souza of Australia. Caplicki introduced

Ganzeer to Booklyn around 2014, resulting in *Trouble Trunk*— a box set of his work published in 2015; it includes a pamphlet with a manifesto by the artist, fourteen posters, stickers, false money, a USB flash drive, and a trade hardcover book titled *Walls of Freedom: Street Art of the Egyptian Revolution* (Berlin: From Here to Fame Publishing, 2014) that elucidates his and other artists' radical work during the Arab Spring uprising in 2011.

Ganzeer created murals and dispersed stickers, false currency, and surveys. He was eventually arrested for his activities, and this garnered international attention to his art and cause. He has since moved to the U.S. in response to harassment from the Egyptian government but remains an active political artist, with his keen eye now expanded to his adopted country and Europe.

Balouta, 2012, Ganzeer, risograph, from Ganzeer's *Trouble Trunk*, 2015, editioned box set. Photo: Booklyn

As seen with Ganzeer's work, social-protest actions are no longer confined to a specific locus and immediate audience, nor are they subject to the whims of mass-media attention to spread the word. Internet communications, social media, and collectives work hard to put their message out to the people and in the streets beyond traditional means of communication. By encouraging the transformation of political action into art, Booklyn's box-set program provides a vital role for artists working for political causes, supporting their work financially and promoting it to a wider audience. MacPhee adds, "When Justseeds compiles its next portfolio set, I can only imagine that Booklyn would provide the backbone from the outset."[21] Further, through its role as an agent of change within established art and scholarly circles, and ensuring activist art is enshrined in public record, Booklyn has created essential space for a more holistic understanding of art's role in political movements of the twenty-first century.

Democracy at Work, 1990, David Wojnarowicz, screenprint, from *Your House is Mine*, editioned artists' book, published by Bulletspace, 1993. Photo: Booklyn

NOTES

1 In *Ganzeer* (Brooklyn, NY: Booklyn, 2015), unpaginated.
2 Nicolas Lampert, *A People's Art History of the United States: 250 Years of Activist Art and Artists Working in Social Justice Movements* (New York: The New Press, 2013), ix [emphasis Lampert's].
3 In addition to Lampert's 2013 publication, other notable recent surveys include James Mann (ed.), *Peace Signs: The Anti-War Movement Illustrated* (Zurich: Edition Olms, 2004); Josh MacPhee and Erik Reuland (eds.), *Realizing the Impossible: Art Against Authority* (Oakland and Edinburgh: AK Press, 2007); MacPhee, Dara Greenwald, and Mary Anne Staniszewski (eds.), *Signs of Change: Social Movement Cultures 1960s to Now* (New York: Exit Art and AK Press, 2010), exh. cat.; MacPhee, *Celebrate People's History: The Poster Book of Resistance and Revolution* (New York: The Feminist Press, 2010); and Yaelle S. Amir, *Required Reading: Printed Material as Agent of Intervention* (New York: Center for Book Arts, 2012), exh. cat.
4 Booklyn was formerly known as the Booklyn Artists Alliance.
5 Email December 14, 2016.
6 For further information, images, and an interview with Ai Weiwei, see *Print/Out: Twenty Years in Print* (New York: Museum of Modern Art, 2012), pp. 49–59; selected content available online at https://www.moma.org/interactives/exhibitions/2012/printout/index.html.
7 Andrew Castrucci and Nadia Coen, "Forward," in *Your House Is Mine* (New York: Bullet Space, 1990), unpaginated.
8 Email December 14, 2016.
9 *Flood!* was originally published in 1992 and is now in its fourth printing.
10 Email December 15, 2016.
11 Justseeds.org/about.
12 Further details at https://www.ivaw.org.
13 Further details at http://justseeds.org/project/ivaw-operation-recovery.
14 Printed Matter also published a small booklet on this action, *Operation Recovery*, as part of its Artists & Activists Pamphlet Series (New York: Printed Matter, 2011).
15 Telephone interview December 14, 2016. MacPhee elaborates that the influential Taller de Gráfica Popular, founded in 1937 in Mexico City, which has published a number of important political art portfolios, has served as a model for the box-set program.
16 Telephone interview September 5, 2012.
17 Weber notes in an email of December 18, 2016 that some of these funds were used to print a resource booklet titled *Occupy Sandy* in a run of 8,000; this was distributed to victims of the 2012 hurricane and provided practical emergency assistance advice. In a December 9, 2016 email Goldstein elaborates that since then "we've given out 'micro-grants' of around $1,000 . . . to a number of projects that we felt represented an extension of the same movement that Occuprint was a part of. This includes a publication put out by 596 Acres, a public art/propaganda project of Interference Archive, and a couple other small projects. We have also donated to a few Kickstarter projects on behalf of Occuprint. Lastly, we have spent some money publishing two issues of the *Rare*

Earth catalog (which two of the Occuprint collaborative helped to organize)—the first produced for the 2014 People's Climate March."

18 Prospectus, *Celebrate People's History: Iraq Veterans Against the War—Ten Years of Fighting for Peace and Justice* (Justseeds, Booklyn, and IVAW, 2014), unpaginated.

19 Email with MacPhee December 17, 2016. Weber adds that New York City Department of Cultural Affairs (DCLA) funds supported the production of many deluxe pre-publication/sponsorship portfolios between 2014 and 2016; many public institutions purchased these box sets "in the neutral acknowledgement that these projects are educationally and historically important" and often displayed the work or incorporated it into their programming (email December 22, 2016).

20 Telephone interviews December 14, 2016.

21 Ibid.

SOME PEOPLE ARE MMMM MANIACSS

EXCERPT

BY FLY-O

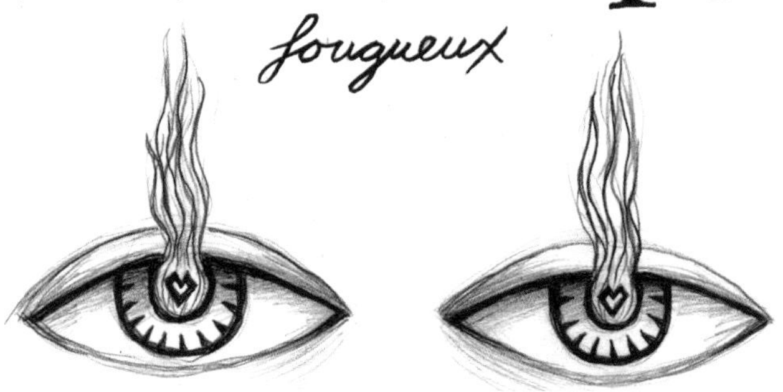

as a BOOK

by FLY·Ø

WORDS & PICTURES... RECORDS OF EVENTS, EXPERIENCES, INTERACTIONS, DREAMS, IDEAS ANGER, VISIONS, DESPARATION, HOPES, PLANS, HISTORY... FACT & FICTION... I LEARNED BEFORE I CAN REMEMBER THAT THE ONLY SAFE PLACE FOR ME IS ON THE PAGE. BEING BIPOLAR & PRONE TO MANIA MY SKETCHBOOK & JOURNAL ARE MY GROUNDING TOOLS - THE MIDDLE GROUND - THE NO MANS LAND - THE LANDING STRIP. IT IS WHERE I AM IN CONTROL, SAFE FROM ATTACK, MY REAL & MOST CONSISTENT HOME. SINCE MY EARLIEST MEMORY I I HAVE CARRIED A SKETCHBOOK OF SOME SORT. THIS IS THE STORY of MY LIFE...

From my earliest memory I have been a "Working Artist"
As a young kid I would stay up all night with a flashlight
Under the covers trying to draw comic book characters
Sometimes I was afraid I would be murdered in my sleep.
So I stayed awake. Drawing.
Little did I know that this was going to be the Story of My Life
The closest I have ever come to "meditation" or a sense...
Of "calm" is when I can just sit and draw
If I am with a lot of people it is my safety net to pull out my sketchbook
then people can mostly leave me alone and it's not considered "rude"
but I do hate it when people look over my shoulder and give their "opinion"
The worst is when someone says "oh that is So Cute!" I don't waste my time
with those people. I hate when people ask me if I am an "Artist"
When your Life is your Art is your Life, that question becomes an insult...

STORY of my LIFE

I didn't understand what my mum was going through when i was a kid; how hard it was for her. She was very beautiful and she did so much for me that I didn't see and appreciate until later in life when I started experiencing the bipolar mania and depression. As a kid it's mostly the scary parts that stick with you and can fuck up your "hard-wiring". I'm so lucky that I got to spend a handful of years with her in a really good place and resolve with myself the frightening things that happened to me as a kid. She died very suddenly on May 15 2016. And now I miss her terribly.

THERE WERE SOME VERY DARK TIMES FOR
when I was really young I used to have a recurring nightmare
ME AS A KID WITH A SCHIZOPHRENIC MUM
where I was with my older brother and my dad and we were beside a wading pond I really wanted
WHO WAS SOMETIMES VERY UNBALANCED &
to go wading and they told me they would wait for me but then when I got in up to my knees
WOULD TAKE OUT HER RAGE & CONFUSION
They both ran away laughing. I was so scared in my dream. And felt so alone Abandonned.
ON ME. THINGS HAPPENED THAT WON'T EVER
I had this dream many times from age 5 - 7 mostly. Later in another house in another city
LEAVE ME PARTLY BECAUSE I HAD NO
I had another recurring nightmare in which I was burning to death every night. There was a fire
VOICE; NO MEANS TO STOP IT & NO UN-
in my room and I couldn't escape. I was burning alive. Not too long after that I got Scarlet
DERSTANDING TO BEGIN WITH THAT IT
Fever. I lost a lot of school time. My skin got red and blistery and I truly felt like I was
WAS NOT NORMAL TREATMENT.
on fire. My mum would tie my hands up every night so that I wouldn't scratch my skin raw but
being tied up was frightening and only added to the feeling that there was No Escape.
NOBODY HELPED ME OR NOTICED. PEOPLE WHO
It was Normal for parents to beat their kids. My mum was Very Abused when she was a kid in England
INFLICTED ABUSE ON ME PRETENDED IT
When she had her first "psychotic break" they put her in an asylum where they put her into
NEVER HAPPENED OR DIDN'T CONSIDER IT
an "Insulin Coma", which is how they dealt with schizophrenics at the time. She also had several
"ABUSE". SOME WOULD BE LEFT BEHIND
rounds of Shock Treatment during her life which always helped her a lot. She would fall into such
WHEN WE MOVED OR, IN THE CASE OF PSYCHOSIS,
Deep Depressions sometimes. I was a kid; I didn't understand and to me it was
DID NOT REMEMBER. I FELT LIKE A NOTHING
just another reason why other kids could make fun of me. She would physically hurt me as a
BECAUSE THESE AWFUL EXPERIENCES WERE
kid but now I understand and empathize that she was torturing herself much more than she hurt me.

NEVER ACKNOWLEDGED. IF I TRIED TO SPEAK
Many times I was so confused as to what to tell adults when / if asked about my mum
UP I WAS CALLED A LIAR & HUMILIATED. SO-
sometimes I would say the Wrong Thing which would not go well for me
I LEARNED VERY QUICKLY THAT MY DRAWINGS
whenever we moved and I had a new school it was frightening to me but the fact that I was able
& WRITTEN WORDS WERE THE ONLY THING I COULD
to draw well was often my saving grace. In my younger years. later as a teenager the kids were
REALLY TRUST & IT WAS WHAT I DID WELL,
not so impressed. I went through some very intense bullying, especially from age 12 - 15.

THERE WAS NEVER ANY DOUBT IN MY MIND THAT
I WOULD BE AN ARTIST. I HAD NO CHOICE.
Even as a little kid it would come pouring out of me sometimes so fast it was scary
ALL OF THIS WAS PART OF HOW I BECAME COM-
Sometimes I would have "out of body" experiences. When I could not take the pain
PELLED TO START DOCUMENTING MY LIFE. NOT
In body and/or mind. Sometimes the lines were blurred. looking back I am sometimes
JUST AS A GROUNDING TOOL OR "SAFETY BLANKET"
amazed at my actions; like when those girls spray-painted the whole back of my school
BUT TO PROVE, AT LEAST TO MYSELF, THAT THESE
calling me a SLUT and a Whore I was Mortified BUT
THINGS HAD HAPPENED. IT WAS MY ONLY VOICE.
I got up at 6am the next day and I took a can of paint and I PAINTED OVER!!
MY ONLY HISTORY. WITHOUT PUTTING IT ON THE
I painted over ALL of that graffitti It was like I was Possessed by a
PAGE I WOULD NOT EXIST. MY LIFE WOULD
Confident and Fearless person I was So Shy at the time and there was a Gang of Tough
NOT BE VALID, Girls who wanted to kill me for (allegedly) flirting
with one of their boyfriends (true). I was scared shitless. It was 10 against one!
my so-called best friend set me up to get jumped but I Escaped! I RAN! So FAST!!
THROUGH OUT MY LIFE MY SKETCHBOOK AND
So Fast and THAT was the beginning of my
JOURNAL HAVE CREATED ME AS MUCH AS I HAVE
Life as an elite athelete. I won many National Titles
CREATED THEM. I MOVED AROUND A LOT AS A
And competed Internationally. in 1984 I got a bronze medal at the World Championships
KID & IT WAS HARD. I WAS BULLIED A LOT & HOME
I could push my body and mind to beyond human limits.
LIFE WAS VERY UNSTABLE. DRAWING & WRITING
Running was like meditation to me I could run 10 miles and it was so
WAS AN ESCAPE FROM HARSH REALITY & ALSO
relaxing. In High School I would run at least 10 miles daily to
A BRIDGE FROM MY IMAGINATION TO MY ACTUAL
Escape "home-life" as well as Training for National Team
EXPERIENCE. BLENDING ALL ELEMENTS; A
in my early teen years was the beginning of Punk Rock which
RESOLUTION OF EXISTENCE WHICH KEPT ME
CHANGED MY LIFE! At the same time that my Bipolar symtoms kicked in Massively!
ALIVE & WHICH DEVELOPED INTO A PRACTICE
Marathon Running is a great way to channel Mania but it can get out of control
OF DOCUMENTING ALL ASPECTS OF MY LIFE
Everything Speeds Up. Too Many Layers Going Way Too Fast! Launching into outer space
AS A

The Thrill of Flight!

MANIAC

And ... then the inevitable Crash...

I have traveled extensively through North America and Europe, on my own and in a punk band. I survived decades of squatting in abandonned buildings in NYC before we negotiated Legal Ownership.
My sketchbooks carry all of the History. Humor and Heartbreak. The Struggles, Victories and Betrayals. The INtensity and the Immediacy of our Everyday Revolution as Everyday Life. Its all there. Open to Interpretation. There is no index or list of definition of terms or translations. This is My Life and You are just a Visitor.

IT'S A MISTAKE TO ASSUME THAT WHEN SOME-ONE IS "MANIC" THAT THEY ARE COMPLETELY DISORGANIZED & OUT OF CONTROL & DON'T REALIZE WHAT IS GOING ON. PEOPLE HAVE MADE THIS MISTAKE WITH ME BUT WHEN I AM MANIC I JUST GET MORE & MORE OBSESSED WITH ORGANIZATION & DOCUMENTATION. I BECOME HYPER-AWARE AND REMEMBER DETAIL AFTER DETAIL. IT ALL POURS OUT ON THE PAGE - RA-PIDFIRE WORDS & IMAGE. PAGES & PAGES OF THE ENCYCLOPEDIA OF DAY TO DAY.

When I am Manic I get A Lot of work done. I wrote hundreds of pages and made a whole new series of paintings and finished a whole collection of new zines and started writing 2 books.
An old "friend" of mine took the opportunity to steal from me when I was going through a rough time. She figured that I would just think I "lost" all that money. She also stole my medication which I Really Needed. But she could sell it for a lot of $$ And I would be more Manic without it which, she thought, would make me more convinced I had "misplaced" the money and meds. Of course she is an addict and stupidly I trusted her with my keys thinking she was clean.
Her life is sad and tragic. Unfortunately I have had to write her off as a "friend".
Another friend who was my best friend for many years and who I brought into my building... slowly over the course of a decade eventually drove me into severe mania with his conga drum playing directly beneath me. The drums eventually took over my brain completely so that even when there was no actual drumming I still had those rhythms pounding in my head. Like a radio. A very loud radio to which I had no access to the volume button or an off/on switch. It was torture! And it went on and on and on until I eventually wanted to shoot myself in the head. A doctor told me that this was a form of mania caused by a condition called "Ear Worm" which for a normal person is like getting a song stuck in your head and it "drives you nuts"! But for a Maniac like me he described exactly how I experienced it; the "Radio in the Head"

Through all of the noise I tried to get it out on the page and kept all of the details to prove that what I went through was Real; That I might not have lived to tell the tale; That there is more than the "One Truth"

That story is a LONG and traumatic one for me and being able to get it out on the page was one of the ways I was able to survive.

AN UNFORTUNATE CREATURE

It changed my life... Betrayal will do that.

People who struggle with PTSD are Not "Full of Fear".
It takes Immense Courage to go out into the world every day facing
Frightening Demons that are not visible to anyone else.

Telling someone with PTSD that they are "Weak" and "Full of Fear"; that they should just "Let it Go" is demeaning, minimizing and cruel. Announcing it loudly in public can have devastating and potentially dangerous results.

I have endured a lot of physical pain and challenges in my life. I couldn't fit everything on to this page. I have done a lot of "pain drawings". It gives me a sense of connection; mind to body which can help with healing and mood. I can also document injuries and conditions; map their progress and interactions which can really help me figure out what is working. Its this feeling of having some sort of control that can make a lot of difference.

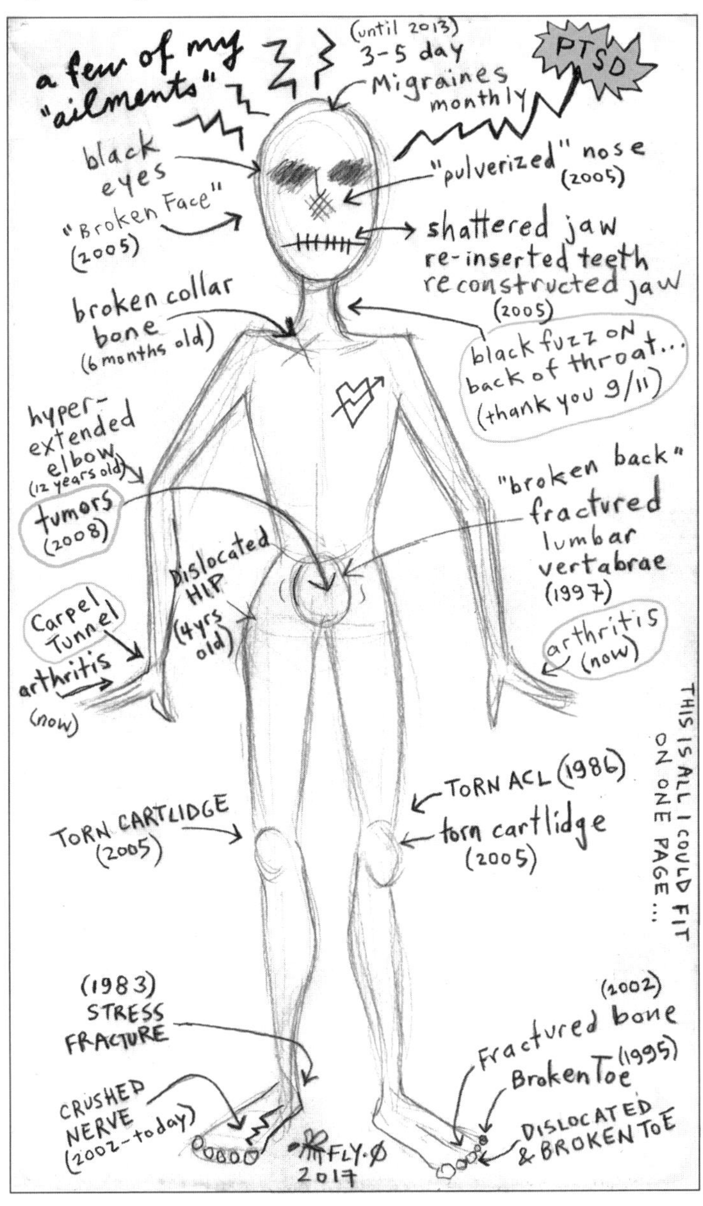

YOU WHO ARE
ABOUT TO
READ

WE SALUTE YOU

KAREN ELIOT

The Root of the Matter

The Artists' Book in the Twenty-first Century

I had taken to the book as if to a lover, for it revealed great secrets to me, but at what cost? Though it demanded more and more of my time and energy, for day by day it grew larger and larger, I never tired of its embrace. Our trysts grew more and more vigorous and soon the book was close to me in stature. As my own thoughts mingled closely in its intricacies I feared I would not be able to distinguish its tale from mine. Worse, my physical features began to somewhat blend with the book's. At times I could not tell its spine from my own, my arms from the book's, and, at one moment when I rested the book on my boot, I could not discern my foot from the book's.

Stanford Howell Alexander, 1913, *Travels with Fortitude*

IN THE TWENTY-FIRST CENTURY, contemporary artists' books have finally been acknowledged as a stand-alone fine-art medium. Artists' books are now free from serving other media, free from a fetishized craft practice, and free from the linearity of narrative text and typography. And they are free from publishers, editors, and most so-called "free" market influence. Most importantly, in the optimum situation, they are free from the "don't touch" rules of fine art. Artists' books are enigmatic, provocative, and confrontational in and of themselves. The art world and some librarians are not yet sure how to exhibit, monetize, or catalog them. The expanding audience for artists' books greatly

Wounded Knees, 2017, Ian Cozzens, Tim Page, Sara Parkel, Isabelle and Marshall Weber, unique artists' book. Photo: Marshall Weber

Who Served, 2017, Stephen Dupont and Marshall Weber, unique artists' book. Photo: Marshall Weber

appreciates the same characteristics of the medium that make it difficult to program: the intimacy, the tactile nature, and the form's resistance to commodification. It's hard to invest in a piece of art that actually must be touched and worn out as part of the aesthetic experience. And it's even harder to invest in a genre that primarily resides in public educational institutions and thus has no substantial secondary market. From the most conventional and ubiquitous of cultural forms, the book, comes the twenty-first-century artists' book, challenging every aspect of its own lineage and tending to be radically challenging in both form, function, and theory. The artists' book is an esoteric and enigmatic anti-spectacle.

The combination of visual arts, book and papermaking craft, contemporary literature, and the use of audio, olfactory, sequential, and tactile strategies is what makes artists' books a vital material medium of the twenty-first century. The artists' book has as much in common with sequential media like print and photography series, film, and video as it does with poetry, printmaking, and other traditional media. It is this sequential nature, shared with manga and the graphic novel, that makes the artists' book familiar to the contemporary audience. And it is its material nature that makes it attractive to the denizens of the digital world. The artists' book is a refuge from the flat digital world of screens, blurs, and projections. It is there when the "net" is down; it is there when one is "offline"; it is there when the "plug" is pulled, it is off the grid. It usually has mass, feeling, weight, smell, and it is focused. No matter what its complexity, it is definite and concrete (except when it isn't, as in the organic decaying forms or augmented or virtual hybrids).

A POST-COLONIAL RENAISSANCE

> *Leafes cometh downe frome the grate tree in magnificiunt wayes. One goeth upon the other as leafes in a booke, the veins of theme were twineth unto wordes and formes that offereth devine instructiun.*
>
> Cedric Malfountaine, 1674, *Olde Sanctuaries en Welles*

The book, as an interdisciplinary vehicle of content and a multimedia object, has proven itself to be as relevant in the digital world of the twenty-first century as it has been at any other point in its complex history. In an artists' book, the arts, humanities, and sciences converge to provide a tactile and intimate experience for the reader that offers an alternative to technological spectacle.

The Internet, email, electronic books, and other digital technology have liberated the book from the practical tasks of record-keeping and narrative-recording in much the same way that photography liberated painting from its more mundane task of representational illustration in the early twentieth century. After the invention of photography, painting experienced a burst of experimental creativity with Expressionism, Cubism, Impressionism, Surrealism, Pop, and numerous other painting styles that expanded both the scope of painting and the ability of a painter to adopt self-reflective and critical practices. After having spent thousands of years looking at other things, painting was now free to look at itself.

By the 1990s the artists' book had transitioned from being a primarily idiosyncratic craft medium to a ubiquitous form of interdisciplinary fine art. At that time the practice was still far ahead of the scholarship. Throughout the nineties and into the early twenty-first century the primary dialog in both the academic and professional discourse about artists' books was focused on the role of craft, fetishizing of material, and obsessive attempts to validate, refine, and categorize the medium. The book has been a creative medium throughout history in forms such as illuminated religious and royal manuscripts, illustrated scientific treatises, Japanese Ehon picture books, Chinese scrolls and screens, Constructivist typographical experiments, livres d'artistes, fine press books, comic books, graphic novels, and zines, yet academic discourse often centered on the colonial bibliophilic past instead of on the present (or the future). The nascent medium of artists' books had not yet distinguished itself from conventional media such as printmaking, nor from modernist concerns of design utility. The book was primarily conceived as being about something, rather than an example of that thing or as a part of that thing,

Central Beijing Codex, 2012, Marshall Weber and Christopher Wilde, unique artists' book. Photo: Marshall Weber

or as being that thing in and of itself. And there was critical resistance to the concept that artists' books could be considered a distinct fine-art form and discipline—much like performance art and video art, two other now sanctified, yet once also novel fine-art forms that also took time to develop both institutional and then popular audiences.

American scholarship and popular writing about artists' books and publications were mired in Euro-centric nineteenth- and twentieth-century perspectives which conceptualized the book as a noun, as material, as an object, or as a container for conventional and traditional dominant media and literature. The curriculum of the most rare book schools, academic book arts programs, and other bibliophilic organizations' programming was predominantly exclusionary, backwards-looking, and primarily rooted in patriarchal, heteronormative, Caucasian, and Judeo-Christian notions of culture, craft, and function. The Bible in all its manifestations was deemed the ultimate artists' book, and a ubiquitous obsession with British and European colonial literature and art was the primary art-historical context and canon for the field. Private, exclusive, competitive, membership-only, commercial antiquarian bookselling associations had almost complete curatorial control over the distribution of artists' books to the academic and bibliophilic market and mirrored and regulated this colonial academic perspective. Thus the scholarship supported the commercial market. (Nothing new here.) Popular artists' book forms and activist and politically informed artists' books were primarily ignored by this dominant culture until increasing numbers of book dealers and—when distribution possibilities decentralized and proliferated beyond the traditional bookstore—book fairs and academic conference circuits realized they could monetize political and alternative publications.

Ironically there was an extreme tendency for the American private bookselling and academic book arts community in the twentieth century to parallel conservative pedagogies about art, which were anti-intellectual and anti-theory and often focused on Western notions of material, design, and craft excellence, diminishing the value of subject matter, diversity, and aesthetics. I exaggerate for effect, but within the public and university library system, Special Collection libraries were often hidden cabals (primarily directed by white Anglophile men), typically stocked by standing orders from private fine presses that seemed only to reprint the aforementioned Bibles and colonial literature and illustration over and over again. The bibliophilic culture was imprisoned in the impregnable nineteenth-century mirrored bubble of hegemonic colonialism and white supremacy.

This all changed in the early twenty-first century as the crucial paradigm shift in the status of artists' books began taking place in the academic, book-dealing, library, and art worlds. Pioneering and persevering through the decades, organizations like Printed Matter, Art Metropole, Boekie Woekie, the Center for Book Arts, and Booklyn worked with visionary artists, collectors, curators, educators, dealers, and librarians and built a global audience for artists' books. The term artists' book and its function and status as a distinct contemporary fine art form entered the public domain at the end of the second millennium.

The exclusively antiquarian librarians at the gates have been replaced by their younger multidisciplinary peers. The gates have been swung wide open by the democratizing force of online catalogs and the progressive pedagogies of modern librarians—who had gained political power and resources as they also became the crucially needed information technology wranglers of the deluge of data that washes through modern academic institutions. Many public and university libraries now have diversity librarians, cultural safety programs, freedom of speech protocols, media literacy programs, public

Spectrum Theory, 2018, Marshall Weber, unique artists' book. Photo: Marshall Weber

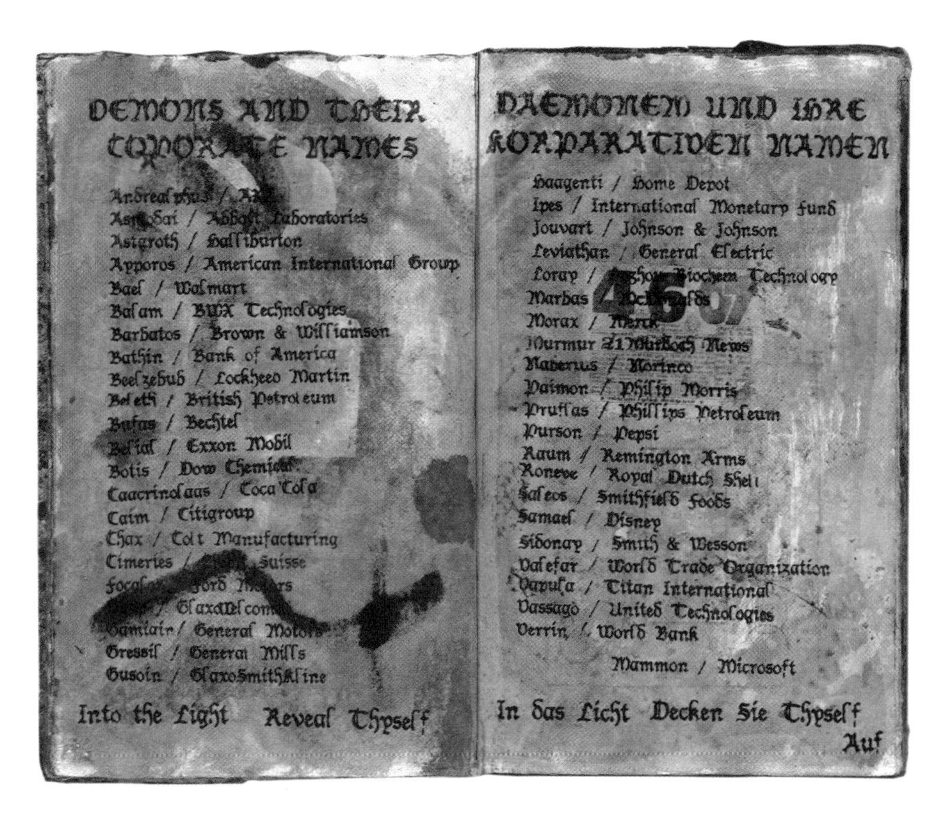

The Bible in Hell, 2008, Kurt Allerslev, Veronika Schäpers, Marshall Weber, Christopher Wilde, and Zon, unique artists' book. Photo: Marshall Weber

outreach programs, and active artists' book and zine collections. There has been a revival of both university and library presses. Special Collection libraries have become cultural and social centers for both students and the general public, with world-class galleries and exhibitions (often featuring artists' books), study lounges, cafés, and event spaces. Artists' books and zines are defined as primary and secondary research materials and have been incorporated into curricula across all disciplines. The decentralization of publishing and distribution has diminished the control of the antiquarian book-dealer associations and broken the lock of standing orders. The contemporary popular renaissance of the artists' book has begun.

Other recent generational shifts, the glacial (and, perhaps, inevitable) diversification of academic and library executive staffs, and the fact that informed students are demanding more inclusive, effective, and progressive materials, have cultured a post-colonial

Street Our Street, 2013, Dana Smith, Daisy Zamorra, Rigo23, and Marshall Weber, editioned artists' book. Photo: Dana Smith

antidote for the colonial malady. Current practice and scholarship have moved artists' books into the twenty-first century, redefining the book as a verb, a process, a dialog, and a performance with myriad hybrid forms. This paradigm shift has reconceptualized creative bookmaking as an inclusive social practice, reflective of and relevant to the diverse global constituency of makers and readers. We don't need or desire to forget or deny the brilliance of the Korans of Herat or the Bibles of Nuremberg, or even (especially?) the hundreds of fine press versions of *Alice in Wonderland*; we just need to acknowledge the rest of our shared bibliophilic cultures as well.

META-CRITICAL PERSPECTIVES

The codex is the diamond of human culture. While maintaining its basic and ergonomically efficient form for more than one thousand years its facets have reflected millions of illuminating social and scientific experiences. The variations of its form are myriad. As the diamond is formed by immense pressure upon carbon (the basic building block of organic life), similarly the codex is formed by the weight of language and art on thought, (the basis of human culture) and often, quite literally, by the force of the printing press. Each page of the codex is a diamond leaf, with a diverse array of interpretations, shining brightly into our mind's eye.

In function the codex is a random access machine. Its linearity is a social construct, not a physical one; you can open a book at any page. And from the analog structure of the codex comes the underlying organizing principles of the Internet, namely the webpage and the scroll and conceptually the concept of random access. And beyond the structure of the codex is the organizing meta-structure of the global library network which forms the overarching analogical neural network that is precedential to the Internet itself.

Dr. Ahed Ashrawi, 1997, *The Fractal Structures of Human Culture*

By the early twenty-first century, the momentum of the artists' book renaissance had drawn the attention of the library world and the art world. As public and academic libraries collected more digital media and fewer printed books, artists' books became one of the fastest-growing areas of material book-collecting. Art and Special Collections libraries have shifted from antiquarian-driven acquisitions focused on bindings and printing examples to subject- and curriculum-based collecting of artists' books and zines and the preservation of the last archives of pre-digital material culture. In an inversion of the past taxonomy, fine press books, livres d'artistes, and other creative book forms that once stood alone and sometimes above artists' books in the genre hierarchy have became subsets of the artists' books genre, now the dominant overarching popular term.

On Evaluating Black Privilege, 2017, CUBA (Clarence Robbs), Crystal Valentine, and Marshall Weber, unique and editioned artists' books. Photo: Marshall Weber

vilege is
hat if I die
Sharpton
e To My fun
sT Al Sharp
ason-jar
s Tears,

New conservation, documentation, and exhibition practices, and Internet library catalogs have taken both antiquarian rare books and artists' books out of obscurity and brought them into the spotlight. Artists' books integrate data with emotion, aesthetics, and material form in a way that provides opportunity for self-reflection and self-critique.

In her influential article in the September 21, 2003 issue of *RBM: A Journal of Rare Books, Manuscripts, and Cultural Heritage*, director of Wesleyan University Special Collections and Archives (and contributor to this book) Suzy Taraba observes, "Artists' books often force the reader to think about the very act of reading and how it is influenced by a variety of factors beyond the text itself." Paralleling the shift in how to classify artists' books, the theoretical discourse surrounding them has also moved from the modernist fixation on absolutes and utility to the inclusion of post-modern concerns of subject matter, function, and fluidity.

In his essay later in this book, first published in the *Artist's Book Yearbook 2006–2007* (Bristol, U.K.: University of the West of England), German artist Anton Würth provides a succinct theoretical substantiation of why artists' books are important to a global human culture created primarily by language and its attendant economic systems. I paraphrase: " . . . the book as an art form does not represent a given content in the (semiotic) affirmative. It is not bound by recognizable forms of (linguistic or typographical) standardization. The artist's book does not intend to be a substitute for the book in its (conventional) practical form, it coexists with (conventional) books as a locus of dissent." Würth proposes that artists' books can function as tools with which to examine where conventional language and content have failed us and how we might alleviate the damage done by that failure with a committed creative investigation of the primary traditional vehicle of written language, the book. In the making of an artists' book, the artist does just this: interfering with the linear structure of the book and the language, and experimenting with the integration of image and printed or written text in ways that are constantly fruitful and challenging. This experimentation is part of the developmental process of new systems of linguistic and visual communication, and these new language systems are needed to assist in resolving current global social and environmental problems. As American linguist Benjamin Lee Whorf theorized, values embedded in the classic language systems may be part of systemic miscommunication problems. Artists and writers who are challenging conventional language may hold keys to more efficient and efficacious means of problem-solving communications.

ART-WORLD VALIDATION

> *The human brain processes image and text through extremely different neurological and cognitive systems. The areas of the brain used for processing images have an ancient evolutionary lineage. The areas used for reading, were, in evolutionary terms, just recently cobbled together from parts of the brain not directly associated with each other until the influence of human language both written and spoken produced these associations.*
>
> Dr. Miriam Lumumba, 2009, *Evolution and Creativity*

By the late 1990s four cultural shifts in the art world had accelerated the changing attitudes towards artists' books and brought them to the attention of the global art audience. While there are various examples of artists using less expensive printing processes in the early and mid twentieth century to produce what would later be defined as artists' books, these projects tended to be undervalued and underacknowledged. Without a popular or theoretical context, these publications were treated as exceptional novelties. The first shift was ideological. In the rapidly expanding, globalized, and politicized contemporary art world of the 1980s, artists developed independent attitudes and sought to have greater or even full control over the production, exhibition, and distribution of their artwork. Combined with the greater financial resources of an expanding contemporary art market, artists were inspired and able to make their own books without interference from the dealers, galleries, presses, and publishers that had limited their book and exhibition catalog projects in the past.

Second, the desktop-printing revolution came to artists' attention. With a personal computer and an ink-jet printer you could make your own books and edition them at a fraction of what it would have cost just a few years earlier. Desktop publishing and the rising quality and affordability of digital printing (including the recent ability of digital copy machines to print on high-quality and handmade papers) created a whole new generation of self-publishers. In the 1990s, experiments with desktop publishing advanced, and artists started incorporating traditional bookmaking media and practices into their desktop-publishing projects. This spurred the proliferation of various hybrid art forms using traditional and digital media. Digital tools, such as digitally produced silkscreen and polymer plates, actually made the use of mechanical printing presses more efficient and flexible and ignited a flurry of letterpress, relief-print, and

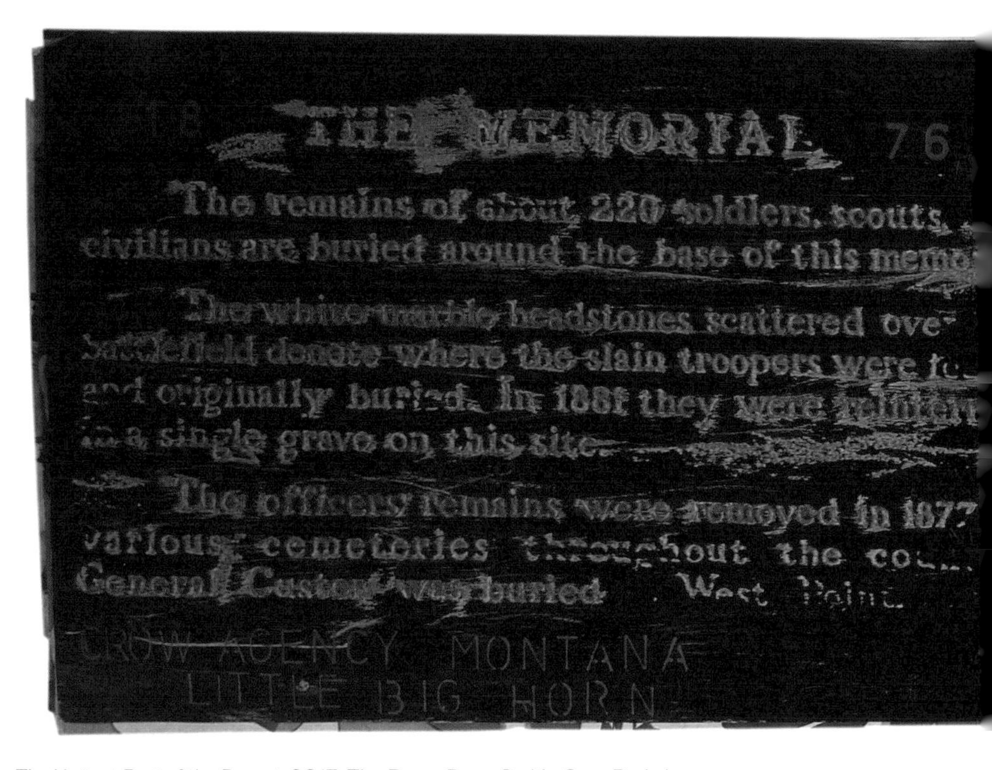

The Hottest Part of the Desert, 2017, Tim Page, Dana Smith, Sara Parkel, Isabelle and Marshall Weber, unique artists' book. Photo: Marshall Weber

silkscreen (serigraphy) printing. This phenomenon saved hundreds of magnificent printing presses from rust and oblivion.

The crude desktop press gave way to the high-tech digital studio press. Sophisticated communities of bookmakers and printmakers were created, sometimes literally overnight. These communities consisted of proprietors of small and fine traditional and analog presses, as well as serious artists who incorporated artists' books as one of the products of their professional multi-disciplinary practice. University art departments, especially in the United States, Britain and Germany, responded to this situation by creating dozens of book art, print-media, and artists' bookmaking programs. By the early 2000s, ink-jet printed artworks and artists' books met and surpassed the rigorous critical standards of the eyes and minds of museum curators, art critics, art collectors, and (perhaps most importantly) popular audiences.

Two other recent art movements prompted more and more visual artists to consider the book as a fine-art medium. The Text/Image movement of the 1980s had some of its origins in the popular political art movements of that same decade. But it was also catalyzed by artists suddenly seeing the limitations of language in a global culture. In the

1990s, innovations in literature and discoveries in the medical and linguistic sciences of vision and hearing had a great impact on artists, motivating many of them to experiment more broadly with text and language in their artworks.

The recent leaps in imaging technologies, such as Functional Magnetic Resonance Imaging (fMRI), which can visually represent how thought travels through the brain, along with current research in cognitive and neurological science, is revealing how we read, write, see, and hear. Many of these discoveries point to reading and writing as being a culturally produced phenomenon, not an organic one. These discoveries intrigued many artists and led to aesthetic investigations of language and vision which continue to build on the achievements of the Text/Image movement.

The Works on Paper movement of the 1980s and 1990s was at first a continuation of the populist political movements of both the 1960s and 1980s when many artists were politicized by global events and started making multiples, posters, books, broadsides, flyers, newspapers, and other more democratic forms of artwork. The Works on Paper movement was also, in part, a reaction to the bloated budgets of art-star celebrities,

art fairs and commercial galleries that were producing huge sculptures, gargantuan photographs, extravagant Disneyland-like installations, and vacuous Hollywood-scale video and film works in the late twentieth and early twenty-first centuries. It was apparent that the money bombs being dropped on these mega-artworks were funneled into the art world by corporate investors and collectors in order to develop contemporary art as a global investment commodity and to create an unregulated art market that could serve as a both a tax shelter and a drug and arms-dealing money laundry. (Numerous documents from the 2016 Panama Papers/ Mossack Fonseca Wikileaks support this observation.) The spectacular art, speculative acquisitions, and machine-fabricated, factory-assembled art behemoths repulsed many younger artists and their audiences, making inevitable a cultural exploration of the opposite.

So in reaction, and in disinterest, many artists started to work on paper, investigating the production of more hands-on, personal and small-scale artworks. Collage, drawing, prints, artists' books, sequential media composed of hand-drawn elements, found and recycled materials, street performance, and other intimate, accessible, and often sustainable

Nor for the Towering Dead, 2017, Mark Cochran, Dana Smith, and Marshall Weber, unique artists' book. Photo: Marshall Weber

materials and media soon corrected the balance of scale that the mega-art monsters had disrupted. Constantly evolving, the artists' book medium fit perfectly into the Works on Paper movement's aesthetic, formal, and material concerns.

Sooner or later the art world follows the artists. Ten years ago a torrent of museum exhibitions featuring artists' books started, and there is no sign it is ending anytime soon. Blockbuster exhibits of artists' books, such as the Brooklyn Museum's *Artists Books* (2000); the New York Public Library's *Ehon: The Artist and the Book in Japanese* (2006); the Museum of Modern Art's *The Russian Avant-Garde Book* (2002) and *Eye on Europe* (2006); the Frankfurt Museum of Applied Art's *Mangamania, Comic-Kultur in Japan 1800–2008*; the Victoria and Albert Museum's *Blood on Paper* (2008); the Walker Art Center's *Text/Messages* (2009); the Boston Athenæum *Artists' Books* (2011); and the immense *Diamond Leaves* triennial exhibitions at the Central Academy of Fine Arts in Beijing evidence the global art world's institutional valorization of the artists' book as a fine-art medium and the general public's increasing interest and appreciation of the artists' book in its numerous manifestations. Despite this validation, artists' books remain difficult to appropriate and commodify due to their material and functional nature.

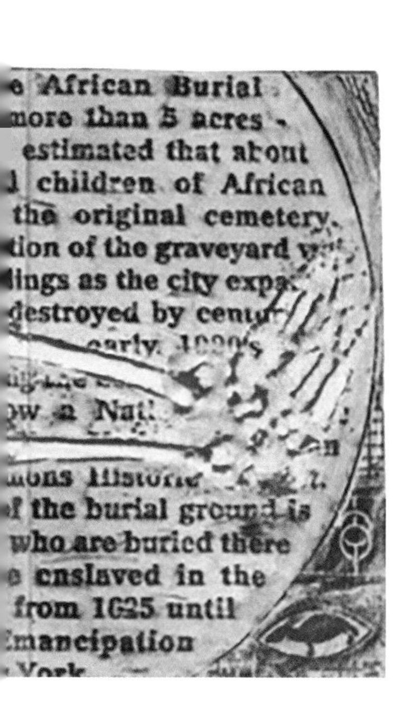

Costly and spectacular artists' books by celebrity artists and a massive injection of eye-candy photo-art books into the trade book market seem to be two possibly negative impacts of this mainstream acceptance. But the popular recognition of the form also has catalyzed academic, public, and art- and publishing-world support for the medium. Meanwhile the artists' books continue to mutate creatively in a diverse, fractal, and decentralized manner. The creative process and production of artists' books also continues to mature with a rising and explicit emphasis on artists' publishing being a form of social practice that aligns with the progressive and humanistic motivations of freedom of the press and expression.

INTO THE FUTURE

> *There will come a time when the page full of text is a forgotten relic. When language is constructed of gestures and symbols and characters so fluid that the concept of a static alphabet will seem as quaint (and useful) as a catapult. The book will be a chimerical vehicle for these dynamic languages. It will be infused with magnets and medicines; living organisms will grow in its pages and converse with the reader. Its papers will be formed of light rays and things as yet unknown to us. The only thing that we can be sure of in the future is that is that the book will still be there, cradling us in its arms as we cradle it in ours.*
>
> Sikong Zuang, 2016, *Balancing Encyclopedias*

Artists' books are the design laboratories of the twenty-first century. They are open fields for play and exploration. They are the reverse vortex of the digital world; products of both the rare illuminated manuscript and the populist publication packed with conceptual and graphic experimentation. Artists' books fulfill a nostalgic function; they are children's books for adults, small theaters that one can carry and store on a shelf and share with a few friends; they are mystical, secret, and exclusive.

The artists' book is an idea farm. Design concepts, new subject matter, new materials and technologies grow like weeds in artists' studios and small presses around the world. The material book and the e-book and all the other "multi-platform" manifestations of digital technology are just starting to explore the possibilities of interaction and hybridism. When these interactions and other new media like digital audio chips, magnetic paper, olfactory devices, micro-illumination, and optic-fiber lighting are integrated into artists' book production, we will see still another renaissance and reworking of the meaning, content, and impact of artists' books. The artists' book has been revitalized as a chimera of fine art and literary media, and its potential as a laboratory for visual communication is just starting to be realized.

While hybrid and digital manifestations of artists' books promise new dimensions of creative practice, the tactile element of the book, as conventionally defined, remains an important component of the material artists' book. (Please note that I'm not arguing that physical materiality is a necessary component of a book.) Recent neurological research in cognitive studies indicate that the tactile experience of feeling the paper and turning the page while reading enhances comprehension and retention. With this type of research in mind, we can theorize that a medium such as the artists' book that often integrates touch, smell, sound, seeing, and reading is a valuable and inexhaustible aesthetic form.

There is no need to set up a hierarchy of media while proposing that the materiality of many artists' books provides an antidotal relief to the digital and virtual world of ubiquitous screens and ephemeral projections. Each medium to its own time and place. But let's end this story by noting that when net neutrality ends, when the plugs are pulled, when the spindly metal towers fall, when the satellites are silent, when the grid is down and the lights turn off, if you hold a printed version of this text in your hand you can continue to read it. And if the sun goes down on you and your book, then you can light your own fire and continue your studies.

RICHARD J. LEE

The Queens Memory Project

The Tradition of Radical American Storytelling

THE GREAT DEPRESSION was a painful period in American history defined by long stretches of unemployment, a sharp rise in labor militancy, and severe public distrust in various social institutions. In the 1930s the American federal government aimed to boost the public's sagging morale and malaise with expansive public-funded projects. One of the more significant public projects was the American Guide Series, part of the Federal Writers' Project. The Guide Series employed writers, editors, and cartographers to create portable guides describing major facets of all forty-eight states, complete with interviews from local residents. The Guide Series' original purpose was not only to keep employment rates buoyed but also to solidify a sense of community. The influential program laid the groundwork for national storytelling by collecting the stories of everyday Americans and ensuring they were documented and permanently presented in an accessible and straightforward manner. This populist-based storytelling program influenced generations of similar projects including such seminal works by Chicago journalist Studs Terkel as *Working*, *Division Street: America* and *Hard Times: An Oral History of the Great Depression*. These books reflect Terkel's decade-long effort to document ordinary people's history.

American storytelling and archives based on community history have evolved to serve as a way for the masses and popular movements to create their own legacies. In contemporary times, such community-history-based archival collections have taken on new structures and forms, especially in the digital age. An example of a contemporary public-history archive is the Queens Memory Project (QMP), created in collaboration with Queens College and run by the Queens Library in New York City. The QMP breaks down traditional barriers to recording history by empowering the general public—through easily accessed digital tools—to tell their stories as everyday Americans and to serve as primary source material for historians and researchers.

The QMP's mission is to make a singular and radical people's archive created for and by the communities and individuals that call Queens home. Currently the oral-history collection contains more than three hundred interviews collected from residents representing upwards of twenty-three countries of origin and conducted in English, Chinese, Spanish, and Korean. The criteria for participants is generally open and inclusive. Interviewees are typically borough residents, but also can be former residents or those employed in Queens. Some are recent immigrants new to the borough, while others are life-long residents with deep connections to the community. Lastly, the QMP reaches out to people in the borough who feel that they or their narratives are not important enough. Ever since its formation, the QMP has been a growing collection within the Queens Library's archives.

The QMP started in 2010 as a graduate thesis project by Natalie Milbrodt while she was earning a master's degree at Queens College. A recent arrival from Detroit, Milbrodt began to interview the leaders and, later, the congregants of the Hindu Temple Society of North America located on Bowne Street in Flushing. Over the next six years, QMP expanded to collect personal histories, photographs, personal ephemera, and other records of contemporary life in all of Queens, becoming at its core an archive of the collective "Queens Experience."

Milbrodt describes the QMP's use of oral histories as a way to bridge the gap in social capital traditionally required for American history-telling: "Families of privilege generally are good at recordkeeping. They also have the resources to give records to institutions. New American immigrants on the other hand are struggling and do not have the means or access to record-keeping and institutions. The Queens Memory Project is a way to document common American narratives because they don't require a staff. Our interviews can be conducted by a familiar family member in an afternoon's time."

To expand its influence, the QMP partners extensively with other local not-for-profit organizations including youth groups, civic clubs, religious organizations, neighborhood historical associations, and senior citizen centers. Sizable immigrant diaspora from Central and South America, Northern Africa, Southeast Asia, and East Asia have settled throughout Queens in the last fifty years. Their presence and propensity to create mobile ethnic enclaves have made Queens a primary location for urban historians to conduct research.

Milbrodt says that an important component of the QMP is that interviews can be conducted in languages other than English: "When people migrate they don't have the luxury of bringing over mementoes and photos. Usually families are forced to travel light. The circumstances of migration, displacement, and crossing boundaries means that oftentimes it is only memories that a new American will always have and carry with them."

"Because of a variety of reasons including language, fear, and accessibility, these diasporas have largely been excluded from the traditional channels of 'history-making,'" Milbrodt further explains. In response, much of the QMP's current efforts focus on documenting the stories of Queen's non-English-speaking communities and other disenfranchised groups.

One such example was an initiative with the Greater Ridgewood Youth Council in 2015. A traditionally German, Irish, Italian, and Jewish neighborhood, Ridgewood became home to new migrants from Eastern Europe, South America, the Middle East, and especially Puerto Rico after the Immigration and Nationality Act of 1965. In recent times, the neighborhood has been undergoing gentrification, with long-time residents of color being displaced and priced out due to rising costs of living. Attuned to Ridgewood's situation, the QMP decided to concentrate efforts on collecting primary source material from the rapidly evolving neighborhood and trained students on how to conduct successful short oral histories. The students did fieldwork by interviewing their friends, families, and neighbors, gathering a variety of perspectives. The resulting interviews revealed innermost thoughts, fears, and anxieties about the changing neighborhood, especially with regards to gentrification. The students shared their results at a capstone public event where the subjects and their families gathered to listen to each others' interviews. They also reinterpreted the contents of the collected oral history by taking poignant lines from the interviews and turning them into poems, which groups of students performed at the event. The students also worked together to produce a zine called *Kin of Queens*, consisting of art inspired by interviewee photos, interviews, and their interactions with the community. The capstone event proved critical for this public initiative because it created new bonds of solidarity.

These successful grassroots efforts cemented the QMP as an organization prescient in methods of gathering relevant documents from the community for future historians. By bringing the means of narrative creation to common people, this model bypasses the time- and labor-intensive process by institutional professionals of surveying, collecting, and describing archival material.

Greater Ridgewood Youth Council after-school program students performing oral history interviews, 2016. Photo: QMP outreach coordinator Reshad Hai

In 2016, a Chinese-speaking outreach coordinator, Yingwen Huang, was hired to collect interviews from Chinese senior citizens. She worked with various senior centers located in Elmhurst and Flushing. Funded by an Institute of Museum and Library Services' Memories of Migration grant, Huang tapped into a wealth of memories held by elderly Chinese-Americans, many of whom were long-time residents. One of these participants told Huang that "my memories are the source of my happiness," confirming her own belief in the QMP mission. "I think being able work on this project and provide people a place where they can share their memories, their emotions, and their stories with others, is also the source of my satisfaction," Huang says.

"It is important that these interviews were done because they reflect the cultures and memories of immigrants living in Queens. Especially in our current political climate where immigration is a heated topic, these interviews documented the voices of the members of our community and provided insights about the obstacles and struggles they overcame. Through these interviews, the voice of our residents have a representation in the local archive as well as in the community they live in."

Photograph donors at a Queens Memory Project event, July 2017.
Photo: QMP coordinator Richard J. Lee

FLORENCIA SAN MARTÍN

To Not Forget Twice

Art and Social Change in Artists' Books from Latin America

IN HER 1994 BOOK, *Latin American Vanguards*, the literary scholar Vicky Unruh convincingly argues that the region's canon of modern art developed itself as vanguard, intertwining visual and literary forms in novel ways.[1] Examples of this are the Peruvian magazine *Amauta* (1926–30); the Cuban publication *Revista Avance* in 1927; the 1921 manifesto *Actual 1* by the Mexican poet and artist Manuel Maples Arce; the collaborations between Norah and Jorge Luis Borges in Argentina in the 1920s; and the calligrams of the Chilean poet Vicente Huidobro at the beginning of the twentieth century.[2] As Unruh maintains, the merging of image and text by Latin American artists and poets did not occur in response to a sad desire of copying or assimilating European avant-garde movements. Rather, it took place within a space of fervent cultural activation, which occurred simultaneously with the Western historical vanguards, and in some cases like *Amauta* (whose indigenous activism was based on the *Ayllu*), it aesthetically revived the pre-Columbian social structures as a strategy of resistance against the dominant models of modernity.

However, it must be said that the twentieth-century Latin American vanguard was not the first to combine image and text as a form of dissidence to the Western hegemony. Four hundred years ago, the Inka intellectual Felipe Guamán Poma de Ayala, in his 1615 manuscript *El primer nueva crónica y buen gobierno* (The First New Chronicle and Good Government), which is 1,200 pages long and contains 400 drawings, exposed the deep crisis that had resulted from the Conquest. In so doing, he created a complex cosmology that "[interwove] the dynasties of the Andean past with the universal Christian model of history, [making] the Incas not the first and only great dynasty, but the most recent."[3] Thus, the images and text in Guamán Poma's manuscript depict indigenous people subjected to religious conversion and other forms of cultural annihilation carried out by the Spanish Crown, offering in turn the possibility of *another* system based on collectivity and solidarity as organizing principles of civil society. This early object, an artists' book, is but an inevitable starting point to think of a recurring theme in Latin American art—the notion of art as an agent of social change—and, with it, its desire (that of art) of socializing discourses that challenge and protest against modernity's hierarchies of power.

In this essay, I would like to propose a genealogy of artists' books that encompasses the idea of art as an agent of social change in Latin America, making visible the ways in which they interrupt the progressive course of modern culture and knowledge. I begin with *Nueva crónica y buen gobierno* and continue with *Contrabienal*, a book by a group of Latin American artists in New York in the early 1970s; I then refer to the works of Waltercio Caldas (Rio de Janeiro, Brazil, 1946); Felipe Ehrenberg (Mexico City, 1943–Cuernavaca, Mexico, 2017); Ulises Carrión San Andrés Tuxtla (Mexico, 1941–Amsterdam, 1989); Mirtha Dermisache (Buenos Aires, Argentina, 1940–2012); and María Verónica San Martín (Santiago, 1981). It is worth noting that these artists and their books are only examples that illustrate the issues mentioned above; this does not mean that they hold more or less importance than many others whom, for reasons of space, I had to leave out. I would also like to note that my intention is not to map a chronological development of artists' books in Latin America, nor to define these books and/or their place within the museum or art institution. In other words, I do not aim to build or re-articulate a geographical canon; what interests me, instead, is to think about how artists' books have served—through their multiple and diverse possibilities—many generations of Latin American artists, including Latinxs and Latin American artists living in the United States, as a means to create and disseminate their aesthetics of resistance to the hegemony.[4] Transformation and social change are thus central tropes in this essay, yet before delving into them vis-à-vis the production of artists' books, I will address the notions of construction and representation of memories, worldviews, and communities in the region through the analysis of *Nueva crónica y buen gobierno* and *Contrabienal*.

Before modernity was invented, along with its dark side, coloniality—that is, before the Spanish and Portuguese invented the so-called New World in the sixteenth century—the cultures of Mesoamerica recorded their conceptions of the world on textured papers they called "*huun.*"[5] Those writings—which, as W.J.T. Mitchell reminds us, are also images—Enlightenment Europeans called hieroglyphs, linking the Maya codices to the Western tradition.[6] In this same vein of cultural and epistemological appropriation, much ink has been spilled to highlight Fray Bartolomé de Las Casas's empathy with the pre-Columbian culture and its peoples, celebrating the pathos of the friar and his "horrified contemplation" of the destruction of the codices by the colonizers during the Mayan genocide. De Las Casas himself wrote a treatise on this in 1550 titled *In Defense of the Indians*, responding to the famous debate he had had with Juan Ginés de Sepúlveda in Valladolid in the mid sixteenth century.[7] As is well documented, while Sepúlveda argued that "the Indians did not have a soul" and therefore should be enslaved, de Las Casas countered that the "Indians"—an erroneous linguistic designation in the first place, linked to Columbus's idea that he was in the West Indies—were to be considered human beings, as they were able to learn when they were "educated properly." The Christian rhetoric of salvation and education thus made the Indians humans, according to the "benevolent" Fray. In fact, the destruction of the Maya codices—these early artists' books—went hand in hand with de Las Casas's energetic defense of the Indians. Yet facing what appears to us as double oblivion—the celebratory genealogy of Christian compassion—one might ask if the Fray was not, indeed, inaugurating another mode of racist discourse, this time cultural. The sociologist Ramón Grosfoguel formulated it thus:

> Bartolomé de las Casas argued that "Indians" have a soul but were in a barbarian stage in need of Christianization; therefore, for de Las Casas it was a sin in the eyes of God to enslave them. What he proposed was to "Christianize" them. Both Las Casas and Sepúlveda represent the inauguration of the two major racist discourses with long-lasting consequences that will be mobilized by Western imperial powers for the next 450 years: biological racist discourses and cultural racist discourses. . . . De Las Casas's theological discourse of "barbarians to be Christianized" in the sixteenth century, transmuted with the rise of Social Sciences into an anthropological cultural racist discourse about "primitives to be civilized."[8]

The reception of *Nueva crónica y buen gobierno* as a "recognition of [its] artistic value" did not take place until the 1970s, a gap of almost four centuries that serves as a paradigmatic example of the double racial discrimination proposed by Grosfoguel, as will be explained later.[9] Yet meanwhile, it is important to note that such reception, and by extension the thesis I propose here, does not rule out the relevance of the materiality

Nueva crónica y buen gobierno, c. 1615, Felipe Guaman Poma de Ayala, unique manuscript. Photo: Royal Library, Copenhagen

of both handmade and machine-made artists' books. Rather, what I suggest stands closer to what curator and artist Marshall Weber identifies as the "emphasis" of artists' books. As he writes, "Though the subject matter [of artist books] is diverse, there is an emphasis on: 1) books that balance the use of images, tactile experience, and material form, 2) books whose materials and structures reflect their subject matter, and 3) books that integrate text with images."[10] These notions often commingle, as occurs in the cases here analyzed, as if they could not exist in isolation—this intersection being a central aspect of the genealogy I am proposing.

Guamán Poma's *Nueva crónica y buen gobierno*, which can be found in the Rare Books and Manuscripts Department of Copenhagen's Royal Library, is itself an object whose materiality in relation to the viewer's experience and the subject it treats through texts and images has caught the attention of many scholars concerned with colonial art and literature of the Andes. However, as I have noted above, attention was not paid until long after the book was completed, and after the eighteenth-century Enlightenment. Kant, as is well documented, claimed that by "nature," the "talent" and capacity to "reason" belonged to the "whites," given that in the rational and moral order of the races, the "reds," that is, the peoples of the Americas, were at the bottom of his hierarchy.[11] Nor did the scholarly attention result from the first publication of a copy of the manuscript in 1936.[12] As the literary scholar Rolena Adorno clarifies, the appreciation of this book as an art object and a complex source for understanding Andean culture and resistance did not take place until the 1970s.[13] This means that well into the twentieth century, Sepúlveda's and de Las Casas's worldview persisted in academic circles. As the Dean of the Department of Languages at Cornell University told Adorno upon her proposal to write her doctoral dissertation on Guamán Poma, "the Indians [because Indians do not learn] did not write books."[14] In the context of this essay, in which the disruption of the dominant epistemologies is at stake, it is important to note the more than three and a half centuries of indifference of the Western academic community towards this essential book. In fact, on February 14, 1615, Guamán Poma himself sent his manuscript to King Philip III of Spain communicating his opposition to colonial abuses. Thus, as Adorno has argued, contradicting the colonialist commentaries of the book, there is nothing "hidden" or "mysterious" in the manuscript. In other words, there is no "primitivism," as the Eurocentric paradigm has labeled the so-called "Other." Events such as the Bandung Conference on decolonization in 1955—in which representatives from twenty-nine governments of Asian and African nations gathered to set peace terms and discuss economic development, decolonization, and the role of the Third World in the Cold War—along with the proliferation of postcolonialism in the late 1970s led to the production of new forms of knowledge that challenged modernity's homogenization and hierarchization of cultures.[15] But in fact, dissident discourses of modernity have existed since the very invention of America as the New World, as Guamán Poma's book shows. Guamán Poma's aim was to disseminate and expand his demands for social change in the Andean region, and the medium he chose was not a written letter or a fight in the trenches, but a book—an artists' book.

In 1971, more than a dozen Latin American artists living in New York gathered to stage a boycott against the São Paulo Art Biennial. The Biennial, which had been founded in 1951 following the model of the Venice Biennale, celebrated its eleventh edition amid a burgeoning climate of coups and dictatorships in the Southern Cone supported by the United States. Noting the link between the art event and international neocolonialist policies, these artists—among whom were Luis Camnitzer (Lübeck, Germany, 1937), Liliana Porter (Buenos Aires, 1941), César Paternosto (La Plata, Argentina, 1931) and Teodoro Maus (Mexico, 1934)—decided to create an artists' book.[16] Titled *Contrabienal*, its purpose was to protest against the indifference of the Biennial to the machination of violence in Brazil, noting how the former, which proudly highlighted the country's development and progress, was deeply aligned with the logics of modernity and its hidden side: coloniality. A "colonial wound" is how Argentine scholar Walter Mignolo terms this kind of assimilation of discrimination and power relations enforced by the regional elites.[17]

Also known as the "printed biennial," *Contrabienal* marks a key moment in contemporary Latin American art, especially in the relations it established between aesthetics, collectivity, and solidarity, as noted by the art historian Aimé Iglesias Lukin.[18] Its focus on politics, on the other hand, introduces us to the notion of "conceptualism" in the art of numerous artists of this generation—many of whom made and continue to make artists' books, as will be discussed later. One of these artists is Felipe Ehrenberg, who sees as a key aspect of artists' books the faculty of their maker to decide on the edition and circulation of their work without necessarily requiring the approval of an editorial industry, and, with it, a system of external power such as the art institution.[20] The artists of *Contrabienal* were well aware of this; their book, made of 114 pages and measuring 8½ × 11 inches, was published in an edition of about 500 copies which were distributed at no charge by the artists and their communities in and beyond New York. The fact that the copies were distributed for free does not define the degree of socialization, nor the ethical and political value of the book. These factors, rather, were determined by the book's distribution channels. Traveling from hand to hand on the streets, at home, in the museum, or at the gallery, *Contrabienal* broke through the boundaries between spaces for art and civil engagement, altering, in turn, the normalized and prevailing modern discourse of art. This was a discourse introduced by Kant—the idea that if an artwork was judged as beautiful, and therefore universal, it could make the person contemplating it transcend, *go beyond*. Something completely different happened with *Contrabienal*: the experience of the spectator-participant consisted of becoming aware—an active action within the geopolitics of knowledge—of a localized conflict concerning a resistant and dissatisfied collective body. And this took place not only through the book's channels of dissemination, but also through its objectuality: that is, in terms of the production techniques used and its images, texts, colours, and layout.

The title *Contrabienal* is printed on the cover of the book in capital letters and black typography repeated in two vertical rows, differentiating itself from the red color filling the background image. This chromatic decision refers to "the violence the book would account for, but also made reference to the preferred color of the left-wing revolutionary ideology that many of the artists expressed."[21] In fact, this red has two tonalities: one is darker, and the other is lighter, alluding to the dichotomy between light and shadow, and, in turn, to the relations between negative and positive, original and reproduction. Red, therefore, is not only an ideology, but also a technical item of reproducibility, aligning technique and aesthetics in a single non-elitist, contestatory action. Based on a photograph, the image of the cover represents a political prisoner whose hands are tied to a rope. Several knots are wrapped around his wrists, contrasting the tension of the rope to his tired, aching fists. This opposition between tautness and exhaustion evokes the idea of a time without time, where fight does not follow fatigue nor vice versa. As is well known about the Southern Cone dictatorships, the torture of individuals was not only physical but also psychological, and one field technique frequently used was making the victim lose track of time. On the top left of the cover, we read too the diagonal text "English excerpts in back." We thus learn that the body of the book does not erase—twice—the mother tongue; although it is true that the Castilian and Portuguese languages, along with French and English, were imposed on the region at different colonial times (the first two in the sixteenth century; the second two during the imperial expansion of France and England during the eighteenth and nineteenth century), it is also true that these languages were learned, adopted, and certainly reclassified by the Latin American peoples. Language, in effect, is always a cultural decision.

Contrabienal, 1972, various artists, editioned artists' book. Photographer unknown.

Upon opening *Contrabienal*, the reader observes photographic and textual testimonies documenting the torture, disappearance, and execution of people during Brazil's dictatorship (1964–86), followed by "contributions from 61 artists, and letters of support signed by 112 notable figures from throughout the Americas and Europe."[22] Their contributions responded to the open call of the *Contrabienal* artists, who had sent out a letter to over a hundred artists—reprinted in the book's introduction—warning that the São Paulo Biennial was an "instrument of cultural colonization in our countries, a function that this biennial [shared] with many other cultural activities that [took] place in Latin America."[23] The letter reminds us today that Latin America was for these artists a geopolitical space of intersection, where neocolonial models of domination stood in contrast to those that could be answered through an action of solidarity. Nevertheless, I do not intend here to delve into the well-documented debates on Latin American art "identity," a trope that the Cuban art curator Gerardo Mosquera famously called a "neurosis."[24] Rather, my aim is to show, as Mosquera and other critics have done, the *existence* of a great variety of visual practices produced by artists *from* Latin America, in contrast to a definition of a pure "Latin American art," better named as a cultural construct.[25] In this historical context, it is important to clarify that in identifying with Latin America, the *Contrabienal* artists were not attempting to promote a geographical-cultural entity through a single movement or style. In fact, something that most likely unifies them in making this book is the immense variety of styles and forms, generated, in large part, by the diversity of the contributing artists and organizations. The label "Latin American artist," though, led to bonds of solidarity as well as to the organization of gatherings and aesthetic operations that attempted to share common experiences of domination and neocolonialism. *Contrabienal* is thus an artists' book yet also an action—a collective and solidary protest against the complicity of art with the neocolonial system of power. It is not an artists' book focused—as is often canonically thought of the medium—on its materiality as a conventional object where texts and images are formally printed. By not mirroring the desires of the elites and the fashions of consensus, *Contrabienal* ends up ignoring them. Like *Nueva crónica y buen gobierno*, *Contrabienal* simply starts from that point of consensus in order to face and oppose it. In so doing, the book transforms Kant's idea of transcendence into contingency, the artistic genius into collectivity, and the creative talent into a political and social aesthetic commitment. As the Peruvian sociologist Aníbal Quijano has stated on several occasions: "*Vivimos adentro, pero en contra.*" ("We live inside it, but against it.")

Earlier on, when I referred to the notion of "conceptualism," I intended to stress its difference with "conceptual art," and how the latter has been understood in the United States and Europe. Briefly, "conceptualism," as the *Contrabienal* artist Luis Camnitzer argues, aligns with the concept of "contextualization," and involves politics, literature, and/or pedagogy in the making of and thinking about art.[26] Conceptual art, on the other hand, is more related to the notion of "dematerialization" put forward by the U.S. art critic Lucy R. Lippard, emphasizing the formal aspect of a work. However, while books by Caldas, Ehrenberg, Carrión, and Dermisache stand close to the conceptualism that Camnitzer propounds, some younger artists, such as San Martín, not only consider the legacy of the collective struggles from the past decades but also suggest new ethical and aesthetic approaches to the representation of sensitive memories.

Analyzing the work of Alfredo Jaar (Santiago, 1956), a Chilean artist who has focused on unequal power relations for forty years using journalistic images that represent extreme situations of human suffering, the Belgian political theorist Chantal Mouffe noticed something about the relation between art and politics that Camnitzer's thinking also seems to grasp, albeit between the lines. According to Mouffe, all art is political, yet while one type of art is critical of the status quo—that is, of the hegemony—the other mirrors it, continuing and reaffirming its uniformity."[27] Thus, the label "political art" not only designates such critical art as being just another in the great variety of forms labeled with the word "Art," but also implies hegemony, suggesting that all categories that do not correspond to "political art" lack politics, as if the hegemony were natural and obvious, and nothing—much less art—could interfere with such obviousness. The artists I analyze here challenge that hegemony, inscribing politics in civil society, in the art world, or in both spaces at the same time. Waltercio Caldas, for example, aims to contradict the hegemonic politics of artists' books. "I do not think my books could be understood unless you put them in a general context of the work. I am basically an artist who has a special pleasure for three-dimensional objects. I think with three-dimensional objects it's possible to create situations that would be impossible [otherwise] . . . So I produced books with these characteristics," Caldas said in a recent interview.[28] His books are allegories of living spaces, of experiences, as are his installations or drawings. To inhabit the book is, for Caldas, to inhabit the ever-evaluative relationship with the labels placed on art.

Other artists, however, have melded the demands of the public sphere with those that occur within art. One of these artists is Felipe Ehrenberg, who was also an activist and a pedagogue. In 1972, during his exile in London after the Tlatelolco massacre in Mexico City—when student and civilian protesters were killed by the police and military forces in a protest against the 1968 political regime—Ehrenberg co-founded the publishing house Beau Geste Press/Libro Acción Libre. Its motto, "Our press is not a business, it's a way of life" is not surprising, given the intersections between art and life that took place in the demonstrations prior to the 1968 student movement in Mexico. Politics in the realms of society and also art coexisted in the thinking and work of Ehrenberg, whose own expressions in publications such as *Schmuck* challenged the external system of art.

These publications sometimes only had one original, a resistance to multiplicity that is not a bourgeois or modern attitude, as French poet and art critic Charles Baudelaire would have thought, had it been a photograph. It was, rather, a conscious decision against mass production and dissemination within the context of post-capitalism. Thus, neither is it strange that when Ehrenberg returned to Mexico from exile in the context of Los Grupos, he formed part of the Pentagon Process (1976–85), challenging, through protests and collective actions, the cultural policies of the Mexican state in the wake of Tlatelolco. A network of Latin American artists reappeared at that time denouncing repression and censorship in the region. And once again, the complacency of traditional art was evidenced by the disciplined homogenization of the body, as it had been designed by the dictatorships and their aftermath. Ehrenberg's conceptualist experimentations, such as *Codex Aeroscriptus Ehrenbergensis* (1990), and the books of other artists he published (who were often visual poets) stab the progressive course of "universal" and apparently apolitical modern art.

It is not strange that Ehrenberg was interested in the work of Ulises Carrión's work. Trained as a writer—"One not good," as Mexican poet Octavio Paz pointed out, "from the clouds"[29]—Carrión is a key artist of conceptualism and making artists' books. "Dear Reader. Don't Read" he wrote in 1972, separating the phrase in a diptych, and then making drawings and travel postcards out of it. Yes, traveling around the world precariously is not the same as doing so "primitively." Rejecting the literary and visual conventions of not only modernity but also postmodernity—French philosopher Roland Barthes famously said in the late 1960s that the birth of the reader came at the cost of the death of the author—Carrión, "the bad author", according to Paz, asked the reader not to read. In so doing, he challenged the obedient policies of culture, focusing for almost two decades on the conceptualization, creation, and sociability of artists' books. As Ehrenberg had done in 1972, three years later Carrión founded a bookstore-archive called Other Books & So in The Netherlands, where he lived. "A space for exhibition and distribution of other books, non-books, anti-books, pseudo books, quasi books," reads the advertisement postcard made by Carrión for Other Books and So. And these *other* books, which were significantly different from the Latin American *boom* literature and traditional arts, were later conceptualized by Carrión in his well-known essay *El arte nuevo de hacer libros* (The New Art of Making Books). Referring to the problem of describing the uniqueness of the artists' book, Carrión suggested a differentiation between artists' books and book-works. "I preferred to opt for book-work," he explained, "because it frees books from the appropriation of artists and emphasizes, at the same time, the book as an autonomous form and work."[30] The elimination of the word "artist," and, therefore, the rejection of its canonical bourgeois and authorial connotations, now holds a place in global cultural practices dedicated to social activism, as in the so-called Social Practice.[31]

But beyond pointing out an antecedent ignored by these global practices, it is important to highlight the solidarity network of Latin American artists to whom I have referred above, considering that Carrión, for example, displayed the work of the Argentine Mirtha Dermisache in his bookstore. In 1971, Barthes himself, who made his first book in the mid 1960s, celebrated the work of Dermisache, arguing that her books reached the "essence of writing"—the "essence" to which he referred indicating what Dermisache then called "illegible graphics," a removal of the distinctions between figuration and abstraction, and a challenging of the iconic sign—the drawing—and the symbolic sign—the language—as transparent communication tools. However, these interruptions are not formal nor semiological. They are not, in other words, modern or postmodern. In fact, in this context of discussion in which decolonial thinking is at stake, it is crucial to note that postmodernity does not replace modernity but continues within and alongside it. Observing and problematizing the theme of originality in connection to Walter Benjamin's thinking, Dermisache was especially interested in the editorial capacity of Carrión's books, and said that the reproducibility of "illegible graphics," as the Argentine art critic Mercedes Casanegra has noted, "was eloquent in times of silencing the military dictatorship." In fact, Dermisache's first retrospective—which took place at Malba, The Latin American Art Museum of Buenos Aires, in 2017—was titled *Mirtha Dermisache: Porque ¡yo escribo!* (*Mirtha Dermisache: Because I Write!*). This title highlights the constant struggle of an artist—a female artist—to write, and to do so during and after the Argentine civil-military dictatorship (1976–83). Dermisache wrote; she made artists' books. And she always did so in the present tense, subjecting her aesthetic experience to the dictatorial censorship of body and speech, as well as in its aftermath, in its memory.

Diario No. 1 Año 1, 1972, Mirtha Dermisache, ink painting and editioned artists' book. Photo: Archivo Mirtha Dermisache

A young artist who has addressed memory specifically through the making of artists' books is María Verónica San Martín. Born in Santiago de Chile in 1981, her work challenges the notions of forgiveness and forgetfulness implemented in post-dictatorship Chile, planting the thought that things could be otherwise, and provoking a desire for change in the viewer. Using printmaking not only as a technique but also as a conceptual means to explore memory, as shown in her 2013 *Memory and Landscape: Unveiling the Historic Truth of Chile 1973–1990*, faces of the missing ones disappear and reappear. This process—its temporality involving invisibility and visibility—recalls demands related to the truthfulness of reconciliation. Reconciliation's aim, as shown in truth reports such as Rettig (officially called the 1991 National Commission for Truth and Reconciliation Report), is, as the cultural critic Nelly Richard has argued, to close the issue of the "disappeared." [32] San Martín's work brings slogans from the public sphere into the art world, such as the plural question "¿Dónde están?" (Where are they?)—a famous phrase taken to the Chilean streets by the victims' families and human-rights organizations. In so doing, she invites the viewer to connect, in a present made of ruins of the past, with the politics of reconciliation by means of faces but also by means of names and places. In turn, her work with the faces of the disappeared and also her mobilization of those faces, names, and places through print suggests an understanding of memory not as past but as a contingent state of the collective experience. It is precisely there, through the image and its mutability, that her books seek to not forget the historical facts as well as their representation. San Martín thus calls not only to not forget, but more importantly, to not forget twice.

While San Martín's work resists the double forgetfulness of the disappeared, making visible experiences of the victims of the Chilean conflict of whom there are no physical remains, Dermisache, by turning the spoken word into a book, calls to not forget the prohibition of expression and free speech in the context of Argentinian military censorship. The same applies to Felipe Ehrenberg when he considers the Tlatelolco massacre and its aftermath, and, in broad terms, the long and large history of repression in Mexican culture and the indigenous world. In turn, the artists' books of Ulises Carrión and Waltercio Caldas remind us, twice, that the political exists not only in the public sphere but also in the art world. And while it is true that *Contrabienal* reflects a historical moment connecting all these concerns in a collective work, Guamán Poma's first decolonial manifestation, shaped in the form of an artists' book, indeed, invites us, once and again, to understand that modernity and its hegemony did not begin last century with the dictatorships, nor during the colonial expansion of France and England two centuries ago. It was alongside the destruction of the peoples and their cultures inhabiting what would later be called America—that is, upon the burning of the Maya's codices and the indifference toward Guamán Poma's manuscript—that modernity and its machine of oblivion and progress began. The artists to whom I have referred, as well as many other artists for whom art is a tool of social change, have resisted this colonialist forgetfulness, omission, and obliteration, and will continue to do so as modernity continues. The common task within the artists in this genealogy is to make visible modernity's darker side and its continuity in both the civic and aesthetic spaces, so that we do not forget twice.

NOTES

1. Vicky Unruh, *Latin American Vanguards: The Art of Contentious Encounters.* (Berkeley: University of California Press, 1994).
2. Created by the writer, journalist, and founder of the Peruvian Socialist Party, José Carlos Mariátegui, *Amauta* was an avant-garde journal that lasted four years, from 1926 to 1930. It combined Mariátegui's writings and those of other intellectuals with images by indigenous artists, such as the painter and illustrator José Sabogal, who suggested the name of the magazine, meaning "wise" in the Quechua language. Indigenous activism, which took place at the beginning of the twentieth century, was a protest movement concerned with the many injustices the indigenous society was subjected to, and with the social inequalities of the proletariat and land workers. Their claims can be found on the pages of *Amauta*.
3. Rolena Adorno, *Guaman Poma and His Illustrated Chronicle from Colonial Peru: From a Century of Scholarship to a New Era of Reading = Guaman Poma y su crónica ilustrada del Perú colonial: un siglo de investigaciones hacia una nueva era de lectura* (Copenhagen: Museum Tusculanum Press, University of Copenhagen and Royal Library, 2001), 47–48.
4. As it has been recently argued, the term "Latinxs" in the United States does not only encompass the Mexican, Puerto Rican, or Cuban descendents or immigrants from the 1960s, but also a broader community that includes immigrants from South and Central America and the Caribbean. For more on this, see José Luis Falconi and José Antonio Mazzotti, eds., *The Other Latinos: Central and South Americans in the United States.* (Cambridge: Harvard University Press, 2007).
5. For more on the relationship between modernity and coloniality, see Walter Mignolo, *The Darker Side of Western Modernity: Global Futures, Decolonial Options* (Durham, NC: Duke University Press, 2011).
6. For more on the notion of text as an image, see W.J.T. Mitchell, "What Is an

Image?" in *Iconology: Image, Text, Ideology* (Chicago: University of Chicago Press, 1986).

7. Bartolomé de Las Casas. *In Defense of the Indians: The Defense of the Most Reverend Lord, Don Fray Bartolomé de las Casas, of the Order of Preachers, Late Bishop of Chiapa, Against the Persecutors and Slanderers of the Peoples of the New World Discovered Across the Seas* (DeKalb: Northern Illinois University Press, 1974).
8. Ramón Grosfoguel, "The Structure of Knowledge in Westernized Universities Epistemic Racism/Sexism and the Four Genocides/Epistemicides of the Long 16th Century" in *Human Architecture: Journal of the Sociology of Self-Knowledge*, XI, Issue 1 (Fall 2013): 73–90, 83.
9. Rolena Adorno, "IV Centenario de la 'Nueva crónica y buen gobierno' de Felipe Guamán Poma de Ayala." Academic paper presented at the Conferencia Magistral, Museo Nacional de Antropología de Perú, Lima, Peru, June 16, 2015.
10. Marshall Weber, "The Roots of the Matter" in *Diamond Leaves* (Beijing: Guangxi Normal University Press, 2012), 18.
11. Immanuel Kant, "Acerca de las variedades de las diferentes razas del hombre," as cited by E. Chukwudi Eze, "El color de la razón. Las ideas de 'raza' en la Antropología de Kant," in Walter Mignolo, ed., *Capitalismo y Geopolítica del conocimiento: El eurocentrismo y la filosofía de la liberación en el debate intelectual contemporáneo* (Buenos Aires: Ediciones del Signo, Colección Plural 2, 2001), 228.
12. The publication of the book as a reproduction was the result of a joint effort of Paul Rivet of the University of Paris's Institute of Ethnology, and the Royal Library in Copenhagen.
13. Adorno, *Guaman Poma and His Illustrated Chronicle*, 47–48.
14. Adorno, "IV Centenario de la 'Nueva crónica y buen gobierno'."
15. This was the era of books such as Edward W. Said's *Orientalism* (New York: Vintage Books, 1978).
16. For more on the artists' book *Contrabienal*, see Aimé Iglesias Lukin, "Contrabienal: Latin American Art, Politics and Identity in New York, 1969–1971," *Artl@s Bulletin* 3, no. 2 (2015): Article 5; Luis Camnitzer, "The Museo Latinoamericano and MICLA" in *A Principality of Its Own: 40 Years of Visual Arts at the Americas Society*, eds. José Luis Falconi and Gabriela Rangel (New York: Americas Society, 2006), 216–29; Carla Stellweg, "'Magnet-New York': Conceptual, Performance, Environmental, and Installation Art by Latin American Artists in New York" in *The Latin American Spirit: Art and Artists in the United States, 1920–1970*, ed. Luis R. Cancel, exh. cat. Bronx Museum (New York: Harry N. Abrams, 1988), 284–311; John A. Farmer and Ilona Katzew, *A Hemispheric Venture: Thirty-Five Years of Culture at the Americas Society, 1965–2000* (New York: Americas Society, 2000); Cecilia Rabossi, "La XI Bienal de San Pablo: propuestas, cuestionamientos y reacciones" in *Exposiciones de Arte Argentino y Latinoamericano. El rol de los museos y los espacios culturales en la interpretación y la difusión del arte*, ed. María José Herrera (Buenos Aires: ArtexArte, 2013), 191–209; and Isobel Whitelegg, "The Bienal de São Paulo: Unseen/Undone (1969–1981)," *Afterall 22* (Autumn/Winter 2009): 106–13. The artists who participated in *Contrabienal* came from Museo Latinoamericano

and Movimiento por la Independencia Cultural de Latinoamérica (MICLA). For more on these groups, see Inglesias Lukin, "Contrabienal: Latin American Art, Politics and Identity in New York, 1969–1971."

17. See Walter Mignolo, *The Idea of Latin America* (Malden, MA: Blackwell Publishing, 2005).
18. Inglesias Lukin, "Contrabienal: Latin American Art, Politics and Identity in New York, 1969–1971."
20. Felipe Ehrenberg. Oral history interview with painter and performance artist Felipe Ehrenberg, interviewed by Gilberto Cardenas, October 6, 2008, Institute for Latino Studies. https://www.youtube.com/watch?v=z9OmxADmB-I
21. Inglesias Lukin, 76.
22. Inglesias Lukin, 70.
23. Quoted by Inglesias Lukin, 76–77.
24. Gerardo Mosquera, "El arte latinoamericano deja de serlo" in *ARCO Latino* (Madrid, 1996).
25. Joaquín Barriendos Rodríguez, "La idea del arte latinoamericano. Estudios globales del arte, geografías subalternas, regionalismos críticos" (PhD diss., Universidad de Barcelona, 2013).
26. Luis Camnitzer, *Conceptualism in Latin American Art: Didactics of Liberation* (Austin: University of Texas Press, 2007).
27. See Chantal Mouffe, "The Artist as Organic Intellectual" in Lucy R. Lippard et. al., *Alfredo Jaar: The Way It Is: An Aesthetics of Resistance* (Berlin: Neue Gesellschaft für Bildende Kunst, 2012).
28. Waltércio Caldas. Interview made during the artist's exhibition *Made in Brasil* at Casa Daros, Rio de Janeiro. March 3, 2015. https://www.daros-latinamerica.net/artist/waltercio-caldas. Retrieved July, 2017.
29. Felipe Ehrenberg. Conversation with Felipe Ehrenberg about Ulises Carrión in the context of Carrión's exhibition Querido Lector. No Lea, at the Museo Jumex, Mexico City (Feb–April, 2017).
30. Ulises Carrión, *El arte nuevo de hacer libros* (Mexico City: Ediciones Tumbona: Consejo Nacional para la Cultura y las Artes CONACULTA, Dirección General de Publicaciones, 2012).
31. For more on Social Practice, see Claire Bishop, *Artificial Hells: Participatory Art and the Politics of Spectatorship* (London: Verso, 2012).
32. Nelly Richard, *Crítica de la memoria, 1990–2010* (Santiago, Chile: Ediciones Universidad Diego Portales, 2010).

Memory and Landscape, 2012, Maria Veronica San Martín, editioned artists' book, 40th Anniversary of the 1973 Military Coup, an exhibition at the Museum of Memory and Human Rights, 2013, Santiago, Chile. Photo: Maria Veronica San Martín

THE SOLAR GRID!
AAAAAAAAAAAAAAAAAAAAAAAAA
OHYOUSTUPID
DUMBBITCHGET
USBOTHKILLED
POSTERRUINED
SCORC
JUST *SHUT UP* AND PUT YOUR SUIT ON, *KAMEEN!*
RYTOPARALYZEMEORWHA--
MUFL

HEY, LISTEN.
SORRY ABOUT PULLING MY HAMMER ON YOU.
I DON'T KNOW *WHAT* GOT INTO ME.
IT'S FINE, MEHRET
WE ALL GET A LITTLE *GREEDY* SOMETIMES, DON'T WE?
NOT TO MENTION THE ***SOLAR GRID.*** IT MAKES US ***ALL*** LOSE OUR SHRAP EVERY ONCE IN A WHILE. RIGHT?
YES.
YES IT DOES. I MUST APOLOGIZE TOO.
I DID NOT MEAN ANY OF THE *VILE* VOCABULARY THAT EXITED MY MOUTH.
I *SINCERELY* APOLOGIZE.
IS YOUR EYE ALRIGHT?

JUST WHAT THE HELL DO YOU THINK YOU'RE DOING?
OH. HELLO, THERE.
JUST PUTTING UP SOME ART.
WHAT'RE YOU BOYS UP TO?
ART?!
AND DO YOU HAVE A PERMIT FOR YOUR ART?!
A PERMIT?
HEH, THAT'S FUNNY.
I DON'T SEE THE CITY ASKING PERMISSION FROM ME TO PUT UP BILLBOARDS IN MY OWN GODDAMN NEIGHBORHOOD.
YET, SOMEHOW, I'M SUPPOSED TO ASK "THE CITY" FOR PERMISSION TO PUT UP A FEW POSTERS IN MY HOOD?
CIGARETTE?

Y'KNOW,
ZAK. SHE ***DOES***
HAVE A POINT.
HMMM.
SO TELL US ABOUT
YOUR... ***ART.***
YEAH.
SURE.

Ganzeer, 2017

Preceding pages (76–79): Pages from *The Solar Grid*, 2016, Ganzeer, a graphic novel to be published in 2019, ink on paper.

GANZEER

An Early Lesson in Touch and Tact

"I CAN'T DO IT ANYMORE," said Abdul Rahman. This perplexed me. It's not like we were stealing or smoking up. All we were doing was making art.

When I was a child, my friend Abdul Rahman and I started a habit of exchanging what I can only describe now as "mail-art." Although no actual mailing occurred, because that would have been an unnecessary expense. We were, after all, just children with absolutely no money to speak of, our wills and desires highly controlled by the all-knowing, all-powerful grown-ups. And, well, we saw each other every day anyway.

What we did was this: once a week, one of us would hand the other an envelope or small package of sorts. Inside would be what felt like a treasure trove of drawings, mini-comics, puzzles, riddles, and stories. The receiver would then spend the week creating a package in response, which he would in turn hand over during recess at school. Naturally, there was an inclination to up the ante with each package. Drawings would become more laborious, puzzles more sophisticated, riddles more tricky, and stories more convoluted. I recall rather vividly the joy of both receiving and making these fun little art objects.

In reception, there was of course the element of surprise. I never knew what would be inside Abdul Rahman's inventive packages. I could never guess what new things there would be, things that I knew he made just for me. What a great feeling that was. There was also the tactility of it all. The opening of the package and finding little hidden gems in the folds and crannies of paper. One time Abdul Rahman had tiny stick figures at the bottom corner of the pages, which when flipped through very quickly created an animation. This, of course, is not astonishing to us now, but when as a kid I first witnessed it, I thought it was just about the coolest thing I'd ever seen. And it was created by my friend! Someone just like me, not one of those . . . y'know, grown-ups, who might as well have been gods for all we knew.

Such discoveries fueled my drive to hit back with even more astonishing surprises for Abdul Rahman. Once I presented him with a small 3 × 3 inch package, about an inch in thickness. The front featured the Superman emblem, hand-drawn in the gloriously saturated colors of cheap kids' markers, against a blue backdrop filled in with pencil colors. Once the tape keeping it sealed was removed, a man's chest dominated yet another package within. Once that layer was peeled, human lungs and other organs adorned the third layer of packaging, and you would peel away at the various layers until nothing at all was left, save for a portrait of Lois Lane. Which I thought was pretty clever. I might've been inspired by something I'd seen in Science class, but I actually don't really remember, because school was the pits and everyone sucked. Except Abdul Rahman. I never actually got the satisfaction of seeing Abdul Rahman's face when he opened the package, because the opening of packages was something we did when we got home from school, something we did in private, but I got the satisfaction of devising something, of making something that I thought he might get a kick out of. I got the satisfaction of imagining the look on his face as he opened the package, and that imaginary look on his face is still lodged in the memory grooves of my brain as one of my proudest achievements.

One might assume that Abdul Rahman and I were driven to devise this method of art exchange purely out of boredom, but you'd be mistaken, because I was actually one of the few kids in my hometown of Cairo, Egypt who grew up with a Nintendo Entertainment System. Nobody I knew had a Nintendo back then, or even a computer. If anybody did have a gaming console—and those kids were rare—it was almost certainly a crappy Atari. I had games like Karateka, Metroid, and Duck Hunt, where I used an actual physical gun to shoot ducks on my television screen! Fascinating things for any child to experience, but still, nothing quite gave me as much thrill as the making, giving, and receiving of these art things to and from Abdul Rahman. I can't really remember how or why we started, but I remember that once we did, it was impossible to stop. Until, well, we did stop.

How we stopped might have had something to do with Abdul Rahman's big mouth. You see, Abdul Rahman had a sole older brother, while I had two older brothers and a younger sister (and I still do). If you've got one sibling, chances are you two are going to be relatively close, sharing a lot—if not everything—with one another. But if you're a sort-of middle child like myself, you are likely going to grow up feeling somewhat excluded, a bit of a loner, and thus keep a great deal to yourself. Abdul Rahman couldn't not show my sorta-mail-art to his brother or get his brother's opinion on some of the stuff he was making for me. This later evolved into Abdul Rahman's older brother's active involvement in some of the contents of his packages, at which point they just weren't as good anymore. Abdul Rahman's dad inevitably caught wind of these extracurricular activities, which meant that he became something of an additional audience member too. He was a man who tended to encourage creativity (he did, after all, provide his children with ample amounts of crayons and paper, as did my own father), but he soon found that his encouragement further emboldened his children's pursuit of this weird genre of quirky almost-mail-art, and he could see them slowly drifting further and further away from, y'know, real school work. The work that would, over time, turn them into proper career men of respectable social standing. Doctors, engineers, architects, or scientists of some sort, obviously.

And so it came to pass that the day I was expecting to be handed a package from Abdul Rahman was the fateful day he told me that he couldn't do it anymore, that we had to stop. Because his dad said so. Such was the power of grown-ups. A power that soon enough we too would attain, with no one to stand in our way.

Of course, I never stopped drawing, but without a particular someone to present it to, without knowing it was going to a very specific audience, it just wasn't the same anymore. And for a very long time it felt very frivolous. Still I kept at it. I kept at it—probably unwisely—well through middle school, high school, and even business school. And while that episode of almost-mail-art I conducted with my buddy Abdul Rahman was a very short-lived one in the context of art-making that dominates my life, I think I might have learned a great deal about art from it. Namely:

1. The best kind of visual art is not art that you merely look at, but art that you can hold in your hands. Art that is tactile, that you can fold, or flip over, or be surprised by upon opening. Art observed from a safe distance is just too limiting for the human experience, because you don't have to be blind to let your hands do part of the seeing.*
2. Making art for a very specific person or audience is likely to be far more motivated than making art with absolutely no audience in mind. The smaller and more specific the audience though, the better somehow.
3. Involving more people in the creation of your art will not necessarily lead to better art.

4. If something about the art makes you feel like you ought to experience it in hiding, away from the scornful eyes of those more powerful than you, all the better.
5. Never reveal the entirety of your plans to the overlords funding your project. Give them enough to allow for continued funding, but do yourself a favor and keep them in the dark about as much as you can get away with.
6. Abdul Rahman's dad was right: art and career seldom mix, because both Abdul Rahman and his brother went on to become well-paid computer scientists, while I continue to dick around with words and pictures, highly dependant on the patronage of others to do so. Turns out my grown-up years aren't all that different from my childhood years after all. I often wonder if that is also true for Abdul Rahman and his brother.

*Note to museums: Displaying artists' books in glass boxes to be observed from a safe incorruptible distance is not how those books were ever intended to be experienced.

SUZY TARABA

A Queer Community of Books

I'M OLD ENOUGH TO REMEMBER when many young people, myself included, who thought they might be gay/lesbian/bisexual/trans/queer (pick your favorite term) sought the company of like-minded others through books. I remember the thrill of discovering a novel (any novel!) that had a subtext, however subtle, of two people of the same gender being drawn to each other in a relationship that went beyond a garden-variety friendship—or that suggested there was some potential. Long before the Internet, long before the relative popularity of queer theory, one of the few ways to learn that you were not alone was to find someone at least a little bit like you between the pages of a book. It hardly mattered whether the characters were female or male or that a lot of the writing was not very good or that everyone like you died or went straight in the end. The important part was the idea that there could be a community of people who did not think that the happy ending had to involve heterosexual marriage and children or else a solitary existence. Of course, a community of kindred souls could also be found in some bars, but that was certainly scarier. The library was a better bet.

Fast forward forty years or so. Queer people are everywhere—TV, movies, books, online. This doesn't make life easy, but it certainly makes it possible to realize that there are like-minded people out there. The library is still a place to find queer community through books. But now I'm no longer searching for that community: I'm helping to foster it. As a special collections librarian, one of my chief duties, and the one I find most rewarding, is teaching students about the rich holdings of libraries and how they can inspire creative inquiry into any area imaginable. Sharing examples from Wesleyan's large and diverse collection of artists' books is a particular pleasure, in part because through artists' books, students begin to understand how research and creativity, form and content, beauty and rigor intersect. A closely related joy is the ability to build Wesleyan's collections with artists' books (and other materials, of course) that I know will spark students' interest as they do mine. Acquiring and sharing queer artists' books is a new way of creating community through books. It's a social activity, no longer something that has to be done secretly for fear of being found out.

Here are twenty queer artists' books that I think are interesting, presented in loose categories, as though being introduced to an undergraduate class or other collection of people gathered together. All except one of them were acquired by me for Wesleyan University's Special Collections & Archives over the course of the past twenty years. This is a small, personal selection not meant to be representative of the entire spectrum of queer artists' books. Some of the book artists identify as LGBTQ+; others do not. But all of the books have queer content. Welcome to the community.

FINE PRESS VS. THE DEMOCRATIC MULTIPLE

Contemporary artists' books evolved from two divergent strains of antecedents: the fine press book and the democratic multiple. The fine press book, descended from the work of nineteenth-century British socialist William Morris, emphasizes the aesthetics of the design and craftsmanship involved in making the book. Think handmade paper, luxurious margins, classic texts. At the other end of the spectrum are democratic multiples: widely distributed, cheaply produced, often containing politically charged or idiosyncratic text. Democratic multiples became a phenomenon in the 1960s in conjunction with the mimeo revolution, when mimeograph technology put the ability to distribute texts into the hands of people with minimal power and little or no access to commercial publishing. Although not usually widely distributed, zines are a contemporary relative of democratic multiples. Both the fine press book and the democratic multiple are reactions against or efforts to subvert the mainstream publishing industry of their eras.

A splendid example of a queer fine press book is the Arion Press edition of the poems of Sappho. Who better than Julie Mehretu to "illustrate" the fragmentary surviving work of the ancient lesbian (and Lesbian) poet whose work survives only in fragments? A contemporary lesbian artist originally from Ethiopia, Mehretu is well known for her complex, layered, arcane images that challenge the viewer to try to decode

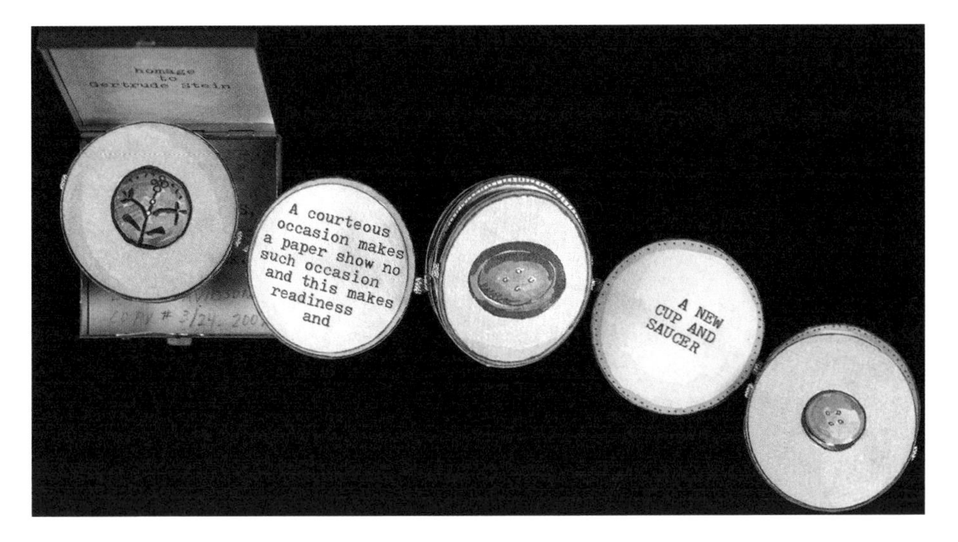

Tender buttons tenderly, 2017, Laura Davidson, editioned artists' book.
Photo: the artist

them. And who better to publish the work than Andrew Hoyem, whose press is renowned for the exquisite beauty of its editions? Mehretu's art is like a palimpsest, a manuscript that has been used and reused to convey strata of meanings over a long time. Reading the Arion Press Sappho is a luscious tactile experience, full of aesthetic, scholarly, and sensual delights.

Robin Price's *Post-feminist Book Titles* is a classic democratic multiple. A small broadside or large postcard, *Post-feminist Book Titles* was printed offset with stenciling, in an unlimited edition, although, of course, the number actually printed was finite. It's clever, political, experimental, and very much of its moment. The text is a list—a spoof, really—of titles of feminist classics, such as *Sisterhood is in tiny little pockets all over the globe* (apologies to Robin Morgan et al.).

RECOVERING AND REIMAGINING HISTORICAL LIVES AND TEXTS

I hope that I never have to pick a favorite category of artists' books, but if I were ever forced to do so, it would have to be those—queer or not—that re-examine an earlier book or text. Here my decades as a special collections librarian rule my choice. Surrounded by books and documents of the past, I am especially drawn to books inspired by their ancestors.

Laura Davidson's homage to Gertrude Stein, *Tender Buttons, tenderly*, is a tiny, precious object that invites appropriately intimate reading. Housed in a found compact decorated with vintage buttons, a string of button-shaped pages attached to each other by a pink ribbon contains extracts from Stein's love poem to Alice B. Toklas, *Tender Buttons*, first published in 1914. Handling the tiny pages and holding them close is a subtle metaphor for the lesbian love the poem evokes.

In *Live oak, with moss: a restorative edition*, Rutherford Witthus reclaims the censored homoerotic elements of Walt Whitman's series of poems from the "Calamus" portion of *Leaves of Grass* using both printed text and reproductions of Whitman's original manuscripts. The meaning of the poems is further restored by Roger Crossgrove's full-page light paintings of

naked men interacting. The photographs are simultaneously graphic and abstract, and they are richly textured and gorgeous. Poet Richard Tayson's foreword provides a twenty-first-century gay context.

Censorship of gay texts is also a theme of *Far Rockaway* by Maureen Cummins. This book is based on a packet of letters she purchased at a flea market. They turned out to be love letters between two men in the 1920s. Before publishing, Cummins contacted the family of the man she could identify for permission to reproduce the letters. Even then, so many decades later, there was still a stigma attached to the long-deceased family member's homosexuality: permission was granted as long as Cummins agreed not to reveal the men's real names. She used pseudonyms instead. The deluxe edition of *Far Rockaway* is

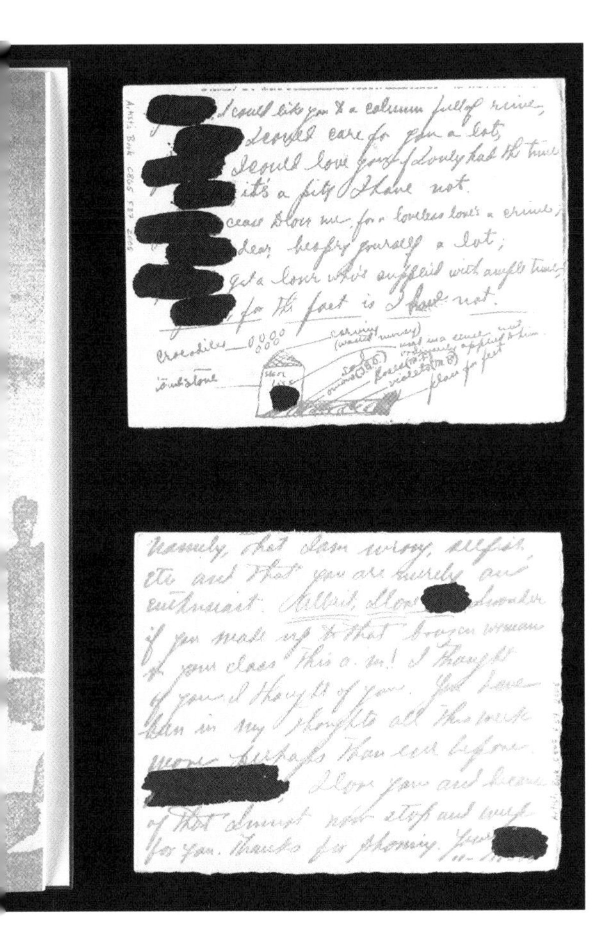

I could like you & a column full of rime,
I could care for you a lot,
I could love you if I only had the time
it's a pity I have not.
cease to love me, for a loveless love's a crime;
dear, keep yourself a lot;
get a lover who's supplied with ample time,
for the fact is I have not.

Crocodiles

namely, that I am wrong, selfish
etc and that you are merely an
enthusiast. Albeit, I love [illegible] I wonder
if you made up to that brazen woman
of your class this a.m.! I thought
of you I thought of you. You have
been in my thoughts all this week
more perhaps than ever before.
I love you and because
of that I must now stop and weep
for you. Thanks for phoning. Yours

Far Rockaway, 2005,
Maureen Cummins, artists' book.
Photo: the artist

My darling, my reason, 2006, Jeffrey Morin. Photo: the artist

housed in a box with a secret compartment that holds reproductions of the censored letters with the names blacked out to chilling effect.

Jeffrey Morin's sailorBOYpress books often take on historical themes. In *My darling, my reason*, Morin repurposes the format of a mid-twentieth-century photo album to uncover the homoerotic desires of an unnamed sailor during World War II and contrast them with letters sent home to his wife. Using stamps, bits of ration books, photographs, and graphics evocative of the era, Morin offers insight into two narratives or ways of understanding the same story. In parallel columns, the letters home (in blue) and the inner monologue (in red) disclose a conflicted identity.

A truly queer book is *M[y] Thieving [Hands]: A story of Jean Genet* by Chip Duyck, printed by Ruth Lingen. Inspired by the works of transgressive French writer Jean Genet, Duyck's text is presented in rebus form. Children were the typical audience for rebuses, which were popular in the nineteenth century and well into the twentieth. Sometimes called hieroglyphics, this picture writing flourished as a way of presenting bible stories to those too

young to read by themselves. More modern versions are often presented as puzzles to be solved. It's no understatement to say that Genet is an author not usually considered appropriate for children, and this book offers a jarring juxtaposition of very adult text and childlike presentation. Some of the pictures offer multiple interpretations; even the title has been read as *M[y] Thieving [Journal]* by some libraries. Hand-colored like many nineteenth-century books, *M[y] Thieving [Hands]* challenges the reader to puzzle out the text and reflect on its intended audience and meaning.

GAY VS. STRAIGHT

These books highlight opposition between queer people and intolerant straight society. Their "us vs. them" stance isn't subtle, nor is it meant to be.

Parallax by Karen Chance is a classic. In a long accordion format, Chance presents two perspectives, one straight, one gay. This brightly colored visual tale of homophobia and its anti-straight counterpart shows two men who encounter each other on the subway. It must be Monday

NO MO PRO MO HO MO PHO BO, 1992, Scott McCarney, editioned artists' book. Photo: the artist

morning, because everyone seems to be going to work in a bad mood. Chance enters her characters' psyches through their musings and their dreams. The straight guy has a nightmare about gay men, conjuring up perversion, disease, corrupting children, and other evils. The gay guy has a parallel dream about the intolerance and unfair authority wielded by straight people over him and his community. The accordion format, deliberately reminding the reader of subway cars, uses cutout windows for insight into the characters and to foreshadow what will happen next. It's not hard to imagine what the punch line will be: there's only one seat left and the two men have to sit next to each other. Is this hope for the future or one more indignity? The reader's perspective will determine the answer.

An early queer artists' book by Scott McCarney is *NO MO PRO MO HO MO PHO BO*, exhibited in connection with the 1993 National March on Washington for Lesbian and Gay Rights. McCarney superimposes images of public figures making reactionary statements against homosexuals over images of young men kissing. The pink paper used for the inside of the book opens out to reveal additional anti-gay public pronouncements, all gleaned from the media of the day. Can McCarney's army of lovers win the war? Reading this democratic multiple twenty-five years after it was published reminds us of what used to be accepted political speech – and how some of it seems to be returning to public discourse.

Brandon Graham's *Tolerance* is another fine example of a modestly presented, inexpensive artists' book that really packs a punch. *Tolerance* uses the very simple format of a single sheet of paper, folded to make a small book that opens out to reveal a larger centerfold. The text is written in the voice of a bigoted straight man who spouts truisms such as "We are all heterosexual people here." Unfolding the book reveals the book artist dressed in cowboy garb, reminding the reader simultaneously of the Village People and of the famous portrait of Walt Whitman that defiantly meets the reader's gaze in the first edition of *Leaves of Grass*. Graham's 2007 book can be read as a more contemporary follow-up to McCarney's *NO MO . . .*, showing how little has changed in some sectors of society. Of course we are not all heterosexual people here, and we never were.

USING THE PAST TO UNDERSTAND THE PRESENT

These books draw parallels between contemporary queer life and the past. Each uses historical material to good effect while commenting on modern issues.

Jeffrey Morin's *The twelve articles: how Joan of Arc and John affect the same persecution* equates a man dying of AIDS with Joan of Arc. Illuminated initials inspired by medieval manuscripts and images of John reminiscent of portraits of saints adorn this beautiful and extremely moving book. An indulgence with a relic of John's hair wraps around the book, a heartbreaking reminder of what may lie ahead. Joan's bravery and martyrdom provide a historical antecedent for the stories of the many men like John who lived and died during the peak of the AIDS crisis.

What does it mean to cross boundaries that mainstream society accepts as fixed? In *Wrongly Bodied Two*, Clarissa Sligh delves deeply into the lives of two people who transitioned across socially accepted categories, drawing parallels between them. The story of Ellen Craft, an enslaved woman who passed as a white man in order to cross the Mason–Dixon line toward freedom in 1848, is presented as a familiar trope that may help the artist, a straight African American woman, understand Jake, a transgender person transitioning from female to male. Sligh uses several genres of text—poetic, narrative, memoir—alongside various images, both abstract mark-making and documentary photography, to tell the stories. Although each person's complex tale is told deeply and affectingly, perhaps the most provocative story is Sligh's own. Struggling to understand Jake's gender dysphoria, Sligh is forced to confront her own prejudices and fears. The tale of the third life is as compelling as those of the original "wrongly bodied two."

Using the familiar format of a wedding album, book artist Nava Atlas views the push for same-sex marriage through the lens of Loving v. Virginia, the 1967 landmark case that legalized interracial marriage. In *Why You Can't Get Married: An Unwedding Album*, Atlas presents a frilly, seemingly traditional album with dual openings that reveal two different but parallel stories. Although this 2013 book very quickly became dated as same-sex marriage became the law of the land, the historical context remains instructive and poignant.

Scott McCarney pays homage to a different model in *Married*. Housed in a sleeve of white netting as though it were a wedding favor, McCarney's portrait of himself and his husband, book artist Keith Smith, is presented one block at a time in direct reference to the pictures of gay performance artists Gilbert & George. *Married* is both joyous and touching, charming and deeply serious.

FORMAT TELLS THE STORY

These books use non-traditional formats to make their points. By playing with and often undermining the expected codex book format, they are queer in both form and content.

Passport to Lesbianism by Lisa Kokin is an example of a unique, altered book. (It is the one book discussed in this essay that is not held by Wesleyan.) Using an actual passport that she has emended, Kokin documents the 1990s lesbian "culture wars" centered around what it meant to be a "real" lesbian. Passport-photo-sized photographs of several women are stamped with labels such as "latent," "dabbles," and "petrified." The result is both telling and humorous, and it equates coming out as a lesbian with a voyage to a foreign country—and coming home.

Married, 2013, Scott McCarney, editioned artists' book. Photo: the artist

Gilbert & George use the flipbook format, which causes images to appear to move when the book is manipulated, for their *'Oh, the Grand old Duke of York.'* In this purely visual book, the pair, attired in business suits, walk down a grand staircase together. The effect is Chaplinesque: jerky movements, deadpan expressions. Are they holding hands? It's hard to tell for sure, but that's part of the point. Without using words, *'Oh, the Grand old Duke of York'* asks the question, "What do gay men really look like?" Now grand old men themselves, Gilbert & George have been queer art icons since the 1960s.

In *El Muro* (*The Wall*), overlays hide and reveal the lively gay and trans subculture that surfaces, mostly at night,

How to Transition on Sixty-three Cents a Day, 2013, Lee Christ, editioned box set. Photo: the artist

on Havana's Malecón. A collaboration between the Cuban photographer Eduardo Hernández Santos and Steve Daiber's Red Trillium Press, based in Florence, Massachusetts,
El muro has a dual-language text and chronicles a population under siege by an oppressive government. The photographs are beautiful and haunting. The format mimics the "now you see them, now you don't" nature of Cuban queer life.

Lee Krist's *How to Transition on Sixty-three Cents a Day* is a collection of ephemera that work together to form a coherent whole. Housed in a film canister, the contents spill out when opened. The narrative unfolds through a series of postcards written to the artist's mother. These are not fancy postcards: they are typical commercially printed tourist fare. "Greetings from Portland!" they proclaim. The other side isn't quite so cheery and carefree. It tells the story of the artist's move from New York to Portland and his transitioning on the tightest budget imaginable. The unnumbered, undated postcards offer the reader many possibilities, some more compelling than others, for structuring the text. What happens next?

Is it really a book or is it a child's toy? "*Revolving gender*" by Benjamin D. Rinehart is both. An object that can be manipulated into several different shapes, "*Revolving gender*" is adorned with pictures of a small child, sometimes colored pink, sometimes blue. As it is reshaped, the object makes a sound like a baby's rattle. This book takes a radical—and playful—approach to what it means to read, and to how we read gender. Is the child a boy or a girl? Who decides?

Revolving gender, 2008, Benjamin D. Rinehart, editioned artists' book. Photo: the artist

YOU DECIDE

Sometimes queer is in the eye of the beholder. Read into it what you wish. *Pairs II* by Aimee Lee is a tiny, sweet, delicate book object, knitted from paper "yarn." Over the course of four leaves, two circles "cleave, drift, separate, and pair again" [from the artist's statement]. Without words, *Pairs II* tells a story of a relationship. Is it sex, a breakup, friendship, one particular night? Is it queer? It can be if you want it to. You get to decide.

BIBLIOGRAPHY

Atlas, Nava. *Why You Can't Get Married: An Unwedding Album*. New Paltz, NY: Amberwood Press, 2013.

Chance, Karen. *Parallax*. Atlanta: Nexus Press, 1987.

Cummins, Maureen. *Far Rockaway: A romantic correspondence*. High Falls, NY: M. Cummins, 2005.

Genet, Jean. *M[y] Thieving [Hands]: A story of Jean Genet.* New York: Picture Books, 2005. Illustrated by Ruth Lingen.

Gilbert & George. *'Oh, the Grand old Duke of York.'* Köln: Oktagon, c. 1996. First published in 1972.

Graham, Brandon. *Tolerance.* Chicago: B. Graham, 2007.

Hernández Santos, Eduardo. *El muro: The Wall.* Florence, MA: Red Trillium Press, 2009.

Kokin, Lisa. *Passport to Lesbianism.* San Francisco: L. Kokin, 1993.

Krist, Lee. *How to Transition on Sixty-three Cents a Day.* Portland, OR: L. Krist, 2013.

Lee, Aimee. *Pairs II.* Hastings-on-Hudson, NY: Bionic Hearing Press, 2013.

McCarney, Scott. *Married.* Rochester, NY: Scott McCarney VisualBooks, 2013.

McCarney, Scott. *NO MO PRO MO HO MO PHO BO.* Rochester, NY: S. McCarney, 1992.

Morin, Jeffrey W. *My darling, my reason: Roger D.N.* Stevens Point, WI: sailorBOYpress, 2006.

Morin, Jeffrey W. *The twelve articles: how Joan of Arc and John affect the same persecution.* Stevens Point, WI: sailorBOYpress, 2001.

Price, Robin. *Post-feminist Book Titles.* Los Angeles: Lavender Armadillo Press, 1986.

Rinehart, Benjamin D. *"Revolving gender."* Appleton, WI: B. D. Rinehart, 2008.

Sappho. *Poetry of Sappho.* San Francisco: Arion Press, 2011. Illus. Julie Mehretu.

Sligh, Clarissa T. *Wrongly Bodied Two.* Rosendale, NY: Women's Studio Workshop, c. 2004.

Stein, Gertrude. *Tender Buttons, tenderly: selected passages from Gertrude Stein's "Tender buttons" published in 1914.* Boston: L. Davidson, 2007.

Whitman, Walt. *Live oak, with moss: a restorative edition.* Walpole, NH: R. Witthus, 2012. Photographs by Roger Crossgrove.

STEPHEN DUPONT

Lost Dogs

BOOKS ARE LIKE LOST DOGS. They want to be found, picked up, touched, and smelt. You know a beautifully printed photo book when you open up its insides and inhale. It is the musky and velvety scent of fine paper stock and rich inks. "It's my perfume," Gerhard Steidl once said.

I wanted to be a war photographer. I didn't want to shoot in a traditional photojournalism style; I wanted my photographs to look like street photography, to bring a Frank-Winogrand feel to conflict photography. I liked the surprise, rhythm, and mishaps that street photography brought. I covered conflict, social injustice, natural disasters,

Baghdad Diary, 2004, Stephen Dupont, unique artists' book.
Photo: the artist

Baghdad Diary, 2004, Stephen Dupont, unique artists' book.
Photo: the artist

and politics. The imperfections of photography drove me to delve into the medium. And the subject matter inspired me to explore making photo-based artists' books.

My earliest books are mostly war diaries. I often travel solo, and my journaling is testimony to myself of what I'm seeing and experiencing; I feel my photographs alone are not enough to tell the complete stories. I write in diary form, taking notes of witness and capture. Enhancing this practice, I also collect objects, research materials, and stories from local newspapers and magazines.

In 2001 the digital revolution took off, and I plunged even deeper into analog photography. My love of prints, contact sheets, film—the raw and imperfect world of analog—drove me to imagine a broad spectrum of photographic practice. I held onto this old world and took it into the twenty-first century with the idea of creating books that would expand my paradigm and my aesthetic. If I could challenge myself, then I could challenge my audience. It was at this time I started to use Polaroid, and it became my preferred film. From creating simple book dummies for trade publications such as *Steam: The Last Steam Trains of India* (with Dewi Lewis Publishing, 1991) and *Lutte* (with Marval, 2003) I moved onto making more elaborate and innovative books.

Over the past five years there's been an explosion in photo-book publishing, from offset commercial titles to boutique fine press publications and self-published limited-edition and unique books. We're seeing a photo-book publishing craze like never before, ironic and strange considering the rapid decline in magazine and newspaper publishing around the world. Decentralized eye-candy production with the masses grasping at print objects—anyone can do it. Global image junkies need a handheld fix: smell it first, hold it tight, look right through it.

Steam: India's Last Steam Trains, 2002, Stephen Dupont, mock-up for trade book. Photo: the artist

Owing to a combination of creative and economic reasons, I chose to pursue the art of bookmaking as one of my main practices. It gave me complete creative control of every aspect of my work, from research and shooting in the field to processing, editing, designing, printing, making, marketing, and even distribution. My photojournalism merged into the fine-art medium of artists' books, and I found an entirely new audience (beyond the newspapers and magazine-glancers) that spanned the world of museums, galleries, universities, art-book fairs, and private collections. By making artists' books I have evolved through many stages. I generally self-assign and/or fund my long-term projects, which all lead to the creation of artists' books. This practice has allowed me to straddle both the journalism and art worlds.

In 2005 I made my first major artists' book *Raskols* (Tok Pisin for "criminals"), a portrait series documenting the individuals behind the faceless gang culture in Papua New Guinea. In the capital city, Port Moresby, using an old Polaroid Land Camera, I shot the entire project on Polaroid 665 positive/negative film. I gave my subjects Polaroids

Raskols, 2005, Stephen Dupont, editioned artists' book. Photo: the artist

Afghanistan 1993–2012: The Box Set, 2012, Stephen Dupont, editioned artists' books. Photo: the artist

as a gesture of thanks and I preserved the negatives in a bucket of sodium-sulphate solution. After hand-printing gelatin silver prints in the darkroom, I glued them together into a concertina book. I scratched and hacked in texts and graphics with a razor blade to give my book the feel, tension, and rawness of gangster life in Papua New Guinea. I then enclosed the accordion pages between stainless-steel front and back covers and made a bolted case of stainless-steel sheets with a rubber interior. The cover and case fronts displayed a chemically etched photograph.

Following *Raskols*, I made a smaller artists' book titled *Sing-Sing* that contains mainly Papua New Guinea tribal portraits I took at the 2004 Mount Hagen cultural show. Again, I used silver gelatin prints and the concertina format, but this time I handwrote the texts and accompanied them with ink stampings from my own woodblock designs and lino cuts.

Don't Look Away, 2017, Stephen Dupont and Elizabeth Tadic, performance. Photo: Elizabeth Tadic

After years of covering conflict and human suffering in Afghanistan, I was searching for a new project to honour and dignify the Afghan people who had been "prisoners of war" for decades. I decided to make a book using all the photographs I took, whether they were good or bad. Through an unedited, honest, testimony, I wanted to honour the event and its people, not my photography.

One sunny spring afternoon in Kabul in 2006, I created an outdoor photo studio to capture people in that specific time and place. Using a borrowed chair and backdrop from an Afghan street photographer, I set about shooting my *Axe Me Biggie, or Mr. Take My Picture* series. This style of photographic portraiture was directly influenced by past colonial recordings and photographs of indigenous peoples. I took inspiration from Mathew Brady's American Civil War portraits, Edward Curtis's *North American Indian* portraits and Richard Avedon's *In the American West* series. I am not an anthropologist or ethnographer, and I was not out to document Afghan people for science or history.

Axe Me Biggie, 2006, Stephen Dupont and Jaques Menasche, editioned artists' book. Photo: Stephen Dupont

With my Polaroid camera and a hundred sheets of film I set up an outdoor studio in the centre of Kabul and invited passersby to sit for a portrait. I chose to shoot only one Polaroid frame per subject. An egalitarian relationship evolved with my subjects as I took the pictures and gave each sitter the original Polaroid positive. Then I placed the negatives inside a bucket of sodium-sulphate solution for fixing and preservation. The ability to give someone an image while you also "take" their picture is for me symbolic of consensus, the contract of respect between the photographer and the subject. Jacques Menasche, who observed the shoot, describes this exchange in an essay in *Afghanistan or the Perils of Freedom* (New York: New York Public Library, 2008):

> Everyone gets a picture. Stephen is shooting 665 black and white Polaroids, one per person. After his shot, he pulls out the cartridge and separates the positive from negative. One for them, one for him. How different this is. Usually photography is a theft, or else, conversely, it is

> commissioned, a paid advertisement. Today it is neither; no one is told what to do. In a place where "freedom" is fast becoming a dirty word, this is a real thing. And it isn't just talk. You get a picture to take home for nothing, so it really is "free."

I was making art more than journalism. The entire process evolved spontaneously and experimentally; I began by trying to isolate my sitters from the background beyond the backdrop, but when events became uncontrollable, I photographed anyway, with crowds surrounding the sitters, and captured whatever else took place in the frame. A veritable riot of willing participants gathered around the simple chair and backdrop as I created a work that challenged the typical constraints and exploitative history of ethnographic reportage.

It was more a street performance than a serious photo session, and as I began to peel away the Polaroids I saw the magic reveal itself. I was blown away by the effect created by having the crowd and environment showing around the edges of the frame. This was a new kind of portraiture, one that mixed directed and collaborative roles between sitter, audience, and photographer and one that was authentic, spontaneous, social documentary; the frame was pulled back, the artifice of the backdrop eclipsed by its supporters. The strength of these photographs was the wonderful gaze of the subject juxtaposed with the spontaneity of the people in the background who assumed that they were not being photographed. Without the instant reveal of image from my Polaroids, I doubt I would have ever discovered that by allowing events to unfold naturally, the crowd would create powerful and emotional street portraits, a series of mise-en-scènes that unassumedly deconstructed the ethnographic isolation of the individual.

In 2005 I created my first digitally printed book, a tomb-sized cloth-bound unique book titled *Tsunami*. My obvious interest and fascination with death becomes clear in this book, and it set the stage for my continual coverage of disasters, death, and themes relating to death.

In 2013 *Typhoon* carried on from *Tsunami* to form the second part of what will become a trilogy of series depicting disasters. My intention is to create books of large-scale imagery and repetition that show the power of these disasters, the human suffering, and the spirit of survival. These are not comfortable books to view: I want my readers to be confronted by and feel something about the tragedies that unfold through the pages.

I had a similar aim with *Panoramas Vol. 1, 1999–2005*, a digitally printed concertina book produced in 2009 in an edition of fifty. Designed around

Tsunami, 2005, Stephen Dupont, editioned artists' book. Photo: the artist

the uncropped panoramic format, it collects six years' worth of my personal favourite panoramic photographs in a kind of visual diary and cinematic journey through war, chaos, revelation, entrapment, isolation, and peace. Unlike my other thematically driven books, this is one of retrospect and survey. The selection of panoramic photographs I chose was based on image strength alone and the sequencing made from pure gut intuition, resulting in a seemingly chaotic memoir. The book's scale and design reflects my interest in 70 mm cinematography; I swapped my mainstay 35 mm frame for the elongated cinema-like frame, allowing the viewer a larger visual field. There are no captions, as I wanted the book to unfold as a purely visual confrontation, evoking questions of time and place and juxtaposition. At the back of the book, however, each panorama image is reprised with its thumbnail image and a caption. Thus all is revealed.

Why Am I A Marine? took another approach to documenting war. Initiated as a personal journal, it became an anthology of both chillingly emotionless and alarmingly passionate and intimate handwritten responses to that question from each member of an Afghanistan-based platoon of U.S. Marines, alongside original Polaroid photographs of the contributors. Their photographic images, their handwriting and their words—often almost illegible—together form their provocative portraits. The images are austere reminders of trauma brought on from conflict, yet somehow they are also restrained. There is hardship, fatigue, and depression, but there is no sign of immediate violence or death. Again, as

Panoramas Vol. 1, 1999–2005, 2005, Stephen Dupont, editioned artists' book. Photo: the artist

with the earlier *Axe Me Biggie*, I sought the collaboration of my subjects. By spending time building relationships with the Marines, I was able to uncover their personal views and reflections on war and Afghanistan.

The Marine War Diary has now become its own life form, an evolving artifact that goes beyond information, memory, or reflection and underpins everything I show, from raw material in the field to the final artists' books, exhibition prints, films, multi-media installations, lectures, and performances. My journalistic philosophy has not changed, but my creative practice and audience has shifted dramatically.

Through my bookmaking stages I have branched out to other media. I discovered that my self-designed and handmade books could also be redesigned as trade editions (*Raskols* with Powerhouse, *Piksa Niugini* with Radius and *Generation AK* with Steidl), allowing my work to be affordable and viewed by larger audiences.

I have had the great opportunity to work closely with publisher Gerhard Steidl. Gerhard has allowed me to have almost complete creative

control of my work. My second book with Steidl, *Locks, Chains & Engine Blocks*, was originally designed and handmade as a limited edition of 15. Twenty years later, I journeyed back into my archive vault and made a new edit for Steidl, incorporating words by Joseph Conrad from *Heart of Darkness.*

Locks, Chains & Engine Blocks chronicles life inside a mental asylum in the Angolan capital Luanda in 1993. I used to believe that nightmares were something of dreams, a burden of one's subconscious, until I stepped inside the world of Papa Kitoko. The civil war was raging, and in between trips to the frontline I managed to gain access to this hidden world of insanity. I set out to explore the traumatic damage that endemic war inflicts on the human psyche. Run by Papa Kitoko, a part traditional healer and part leader of a Christian-based religious sect, the place was so abysmal and horrific, that I felt it was Angola's answer to hell itself.

To document torture is to become touched and complicit in the deepest darkness of humanity's inhumanity, to tell stories that are unspeakable, that no one else will tell; but these are people's lives, and this happened, it was caused, it must stop, and it must not happen again. At worst, these images are evidence of crimes against humanity; at best, they capture the vestiges of dignity in the deepest of human suffering.

The art world allows me to exhibit my books as art objects, displayed on plinths or cased in glass, or laid out in various shapes and styles depending on their structure. The concertina, for instance, my favourite book form, offers a curator many display possibilities. In one exhibition I opened up an entire concertina book (*Axe Me Biggie*) and attached it to the gallery wall, running its entire length. Although I had already exhibited my work in galleries in more conventional ways, I discovered through artists' bookmaking that I could transform my books into large gallery installations as well. This was a major shift in my career. Opening up my books as wallpaper—in installations that allowed the viewer now to literally walk inside my books—provided totally different viewing experiences. In this form, the book really does consume the audience. These kinds of displays drove me to new ways of expression. Books on walls, roofs, floors; attached, suspended, encased. My books now take on various forms and transformations, mixing photography with words, using collage and drawing, printmaking, drama, and music.

The book has become the template for my photography exhibitions, trade books, films, and, right now, a live one-man-show stage production (Don't Look Away). Filmmaker Elizabeth Tadic edited my artists' books, diaries, video, and photographs to music and soundscapes, producing a film that screens behind me as I narrate from my diaries. The performance was directed by Australian actor and director David Field and was supported by Canon Australia.

I also collaborated with filmmaker Krystle Wright, who directed the short film *A Restless Peace*. The film documents my ongoing preoccupation with the theme of death as I photograph Mexico City around the time of the Day of the Dead festivals. It incorporates my photographs using cutting-edge digital

Locks, Chains & Engine Blocks, 2013, Stephen Dupont, editioned artists' book. Photo: the artist

A Restless Peace, 2017, Stephen Dupont and Krystle Wright, video.
Photo: Toby & Pete

animation and music, showcasing my previous journeys and provoking questions around the subject of death and how society deals with it.

Working with other artists, writers, filmmakers, directors, editors, musicians, and philosophers has broadened my own art to some of my highest levels of achievement. Recently I have also been working with artist Marshall Weber on a unique book series, *Dark Illuminations*, which includes *Prisoners of War; Who Served*; *Sought Peace*; *The Lion of Panjshir*; and *Kill Them All*. Weber combines my Afghanistan photographs with wax rubbings and ink painting from war memorials and plaques around the world, producing meditations on war and conquest. In *Sought Peace*, Weber illuminated my photographs with found and cut-up text and ghostly images from rubbings of memorials relating to colonial conflicts across the centuries, creating linkages between global indigenous liberation struggles. In *The Lion of Panjshir,* Weber beautifully messes with my photographs of the assassinated leader of the Northern Alliance, Ahmad Shah Massoud, to provide an enigmatic portrait of this now national hero of Afghanistan, an important and charismatic historical figure.

I've spent a lifetime editing my own photographs, and I have held onto everything: contact sheets and negatives are kept in their original state, nothing is thrown away. Chinagraph marks of multiple editing sessions over the years tell the stories and immortalise the choices. Even my reject slides sit in boxes or plastic sleeves waiting to be looked at again some day, or not. Everything is meticulously archived.

Looking over my contact sheets from years past, I'm often surprised by my original edits. I find many gems overlooked. What once might have seemed like a bad mistake could now be art. My eye for photography is quite different from twenty years ago. I'm less constrained now and much more open-minded, though I'm still searching for the most powerful photographs, the single iconic moments and those that thread a story together. Most of these choices are for magazines, newspapers or books, and I want my best work to be seen.

However, my current artists' book project *Fucked Up Fotos* is not about my best work. On the contrary, it features only the work that I originally overlooked or discarded: the mishaps, the mistakes, and general fuck-ups along the way, the photographs that would have ended up in the rubbish bin. Now they stare back at me with a vengeance, reminding me of the times I opened up the camera and exposed the negative to sunlight, forgetting I still had an unwound roll of film inside. Or how I overprocessed films in the dark room, damaging the negative's emulsion, reticulation, and worse. Double exposures, flash sync problems. Then there are the out-of-date or cheaply made stocks.

Fucked Up Fotos (portrait of Tim Page), 2018, Stephen Dupont, editioned artists' book. Photo: the artist

Fucked Up Fotos questions what makes a great photograph. After all, perfection is boring. These unintendedly imperfect images are usually terrible, but sometimes they are extraordinary, magical, and poetic. They're destructive and layered moments; like a painting they invite us to look much deeper, revealing interwoven fragments of time and space. They are the stuff of artists' books. On my last trip out from Israel, customs officials at Tel Aviv airport x-rayed my films over ten times in three different machines. I patiently watched them deliberately fry my films, and when I processed them and saw the damage I was devastated at first. But I realised

Fucked Up Fotos (Israeli Apartheid Wall), 2018, Stephen Dupont, editioned artists' book. Photo: the artist

the power of their aesthetic: they had taken on a different meaning. They spoke to me of political censorship. They were not just photographs; they were art. And in the role of art beyond reportage, the images take on a more emotive, painterly, and complex quality. They document both the original images of "The Wall"—a prime example of the belligerence of the Zionist State of Israel—and the direct material manipulation of those images by that same force. Life has a way of layering and complicating things. Every photograph is a collaboration between the subject and the photographer; we can't take credit for life itself; we can share it, and we can be open to a wide spectrum of collaboration ranging from explicit projects with other artists to reciprocal and equitable collaborations with subjects and even random and forced collaborations with state power.

Fucked Up Fotos (Beijing, China), 2018, Stephen Dupont, editioned artists' book. Photo: the artist

KODAK
山西网
45
KODAK

¿COMO SE VE LA JUSTICIA
DE VERDAD?
WHAT DOES JUSTICE
REALLY LOOK LIKE?

MOBILE PRINT POWER

Publishing Works through Public Participation

INTRODUCTION

MOBILE PRINT POWER (MPP) started as a weekly printmaking and political education workshop at Immigrant Movement International in Corona, Queens (IMI Corona) in March 2013. Over time, and as regular participants in the workshop began to emerge as co-facilitators and co-organizers, we began referring to ourselves as a collective. We are a multigenerational group with diverse backgrounds from all over New York City and the world. Our different educational backgrounds and viewpoints make us strong as a collective and powerful as artists and activists.

For over four years we have been using our methodology for participatory design in public space along with a pair of portable silkscreen printmaking carts to engage communities and explore social and cultural situations. To transmit the work that we co-create with the community we make books, prints, and public sculptures. Each project that we do reflects our commitment to social justice and our belief in the value of shared artistic production. Inspired by groups like the Black Panthers and the Young Lords, we set out to create a set of principles to guide our work as a collective. During the winter of 2015–16 we wrote the first draft of the MPP 8 Principles (or MPP's 8 Principles). Each principle reflects a particular belief that we aspire to live up to, not only in our work as artists, cultural workers, and educators, but also as students, family members, community members, and friends.

What Does Justice Really Look Like?, 2017, event, South Bronx, NY.
Photo: MPP

OUR PROCESS

Over the years we have established an ever-evolving methodology for creating work and engaging with the public. When invited to contribute to this collection of essays, we began to think more deeply about the role that books play in our work. They are there with us at every public event, they help us prepare and research challenging topics, and they become living documents—some of our final projects. We use handmade sketchbooks as a tool to facilitate the exchange of ideas and knowledge, collecting drawings and writing from the community during public events. We make books at the conclusion of each project, as a way to archive and retransmit the work that we co-create with the community. For us, books are growing, evolving tools that help us engage with the public and produce complex graphic imagery. Below we outline the steps that we usually follow when making our work.

MOBILE PRINT POWER'S 8 PRINCIPLES

1. WE ENGAGE OUR WHOLE SELVES TO THE TASK AT HAND
2. WE VALUE THE SKILLS, KNOWLEDGE, AND EXPERIENCES OF ALL PEOPLE, REGARDLESS OF AGE OR FORMAL EDUCATION
3. WE HONOR ALL COMMUNITY TRADITIONS AND RESPECT ALL COMMUNITY VOICES
4. WE RECOGNIZE THAT DIGNITY HAS NO NATIONALITY AND WE OPPOSE RACISM
5. WE WANT EQUALITY ACROSS THE GENDER SPECTRUM AND WE OPPOSE SEXISM
6. WE REJECT VIOLENT WORDS AND VIOLENT ACTIONS
7. WE VALUE ALL FORMS OF WRITTEN AND SPOKEN LANGUAGE AND OTHER FORMS OF COMMUNICATION
8. WE BELIEVE IN THE POWER OF COLLABORATIVE AND COLLECTIVE WORK

Political education workshop with UnLocal at Interference Archive, 2016, Brooklyn, NY. Photo: MPP

STEP 1: POLITICAL EDUCATION

As a group of artists and activists, we believe in the power of collective action, and we use art to directly confront social issues. Internally and within our community of Corona, Queens we often work with issues of immigrant rights, building solidarity, educational and language justice, displacement, and gentrification. When we are unfamiliar or uninformed about a social issue but presented with an opportunity for a collaboration we seek out opportunities for political education to deepen our understanding of the particular issue. This is yet another way books play into our work. We use them as resources and jumping-off points for our research and for visual language.

STEP 2: RESEARCH AND DEVELOP ESSENTIAL QUESTIONS

Building on Step 1, research plays a critical role in our process as we begin to develop essential questions to bring to the public. These questions allow us an entry point for conversation with people around social issues.

As a collective we generate a number of questions about the topic. These might be related to things we don't know about or issues we want to encourage people to engage with. For example, we partnered with the group Survivor Speak to create awareness around the issue of sex-trafficked and exploited women. We were excited about the opportunity to help this group create posters for International Women's Day but found we had many questions. We also discovered that we had a lot of preconceived notions about sex trafficking. The understanding that we needed in order to break free from our prejudices helped us as we moved to Step 3.

Brainstorming session with students, 2017, Maine College of Art, Portland, ME. Photo: MPP

STEP 3: DETERMINE QUESTIONS TO BRING TO THE PUBLIC

After we've worked as a collective to create a number of questions, we then discuss these with our partner group to hone in on what will be most effective for driving conversation, thought, and action across different ages and groups with a variety of life experiences. For example, in 2016, we partnered with the New York State Youth Leadership Council (NYSYLC) to

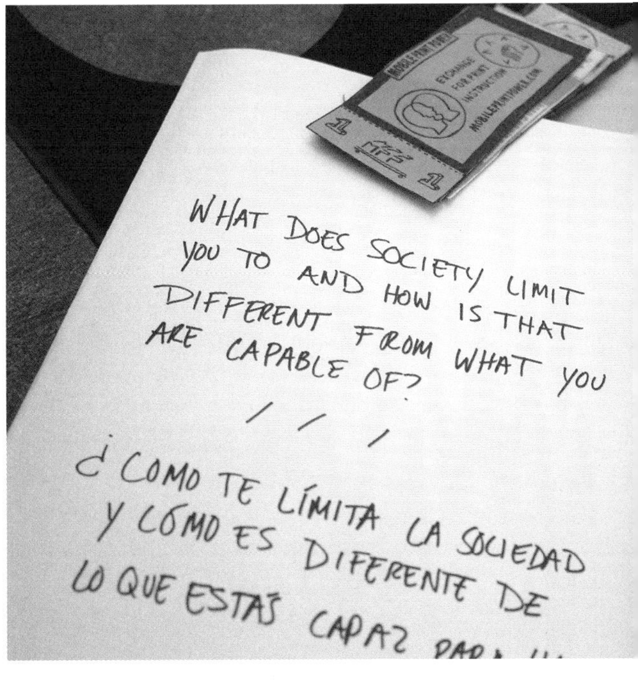

Above: Collecting drawings and writing from the public, 2017, Portland, ME. Photo: MPP
Right: Book for collecting drawings and writing 2017, Socrates Sculpture Park, Queens, NY. Photo: MPP

Mobile Print Power workshop, 2016, Immigrant Movement International, Queens, NY. Photo: MPP

create a participatory project at the Brooklyn Museum around the topic of gentrification. Our question that day was "How have you experienced displacement in your life?" Respondents had experienced many different forms of displacement, from rising rents to forced migration and even the birth of a sibling.

Our questions are also often created with the aim of sparking some sort of visual reference for people, allowing them to draw and help us generate graphics.

STEP 4: FIGURE OUT THE LOGISTICS

This step is challenging as we make all decisions through consensus. We work together as a group or in small groups to make sure that we are prepared for each event. Logistics include transportation, organizing printing materials, establishing roles during the event, set up and break down, and reflection. This is also when we make our handmade sketchbooks for image collecting during the event. Our books are typically 18 × 24 inches so that multiple people can contribute simultaneously and feel they have plenty of space for their contributions. We also create books with hard backing so we can move easily with them throughout the public space and engage more people in the process. Working together to prepare for complicated public projects has contributed a great deal to our group unity, commitment, and trust.

STEP 5: THE EVENT

On the day of a public project, we bring our cart and tables, our books with questions, and our silkscreen materials. We also hang samples of our work from previous projects so people can see where their contributions might end up. This work also serves as inspiration. We engage in dialogue with the public, and we ask them to respond to our questions, with text or drawings, using our large handmade sketchbooks. In exchange for their contributions and conversation we provide them with MPP currency that they can use at our mobile silkscreen cart. MPP currency can be exchanged for print instruction as we teach them how to screenprint, guiding them through the process and printing graphics from previous projects. The questions that we develop and our ability to discuss the issues is critical on the day of the event.

Screenprinting with a family, 2015, Flushing Meadows Corona Park, Queens, NY. Photo: MPP

Crecieno, Resistiendo, 2017, Mobile Print Power, screenprint. Photo: MPP

STEP 6: RECONVENE AND REFLECT

Following an event, we gather as a group, usually the next week, to review the images that we've collected. We break off into small groups, usually of two to three people, and take an in-depth look at what we've collected. We make observations and bring them back to the rest of the MPP group. The opportunity to share observations within this setting allows us to question each other and establish connections between themes that appear in the contributions we've received from the public. In this way our process becomes a form of research. As we carefully analyze the work we have collected, we see how people in our community interpret complex ideas in visual form.

Mobile Print Power members with work from the Solidarity Series, 2015, Corona Plaza, Queens, NY. Photo: MPP

STEP 7: CREATE THE GRAPHICS

After we have made our observations and discussed the contents of the sketchbooks, we begin to develop a final series of graphic images. As we do this, we honor the unique vernacular aesthetics of our community. For example, we have found that symbolism and metaphor are often used to convey ideas of togetherness and community power. In many cases fists are used to represent power, but we also find examples of power being represented through aztec symbols, anthropomorphic forms, and text in many different languages. To create our final series of graphics we often work again in small groups to develop four to five images per event or topic. We then usually present these graphics to our partner groups for feedback or input. From there, we create our final images and produce our silkscreens.

STEP 8: SHARE THE WORK

Once we've finalized the images, we bring them back to the public that helped to create them. We hang the work for all to see, and we print the new images with our cart, inviting further dialogue on the topic. This allows the public to see the work full circle. It also allows them to re-engage with the material, questions, and social issues. Our collaborators often use the images in further work with the public. The entire project becomes an exchange of ideas and knowledge, with the graphics acting as a distributable record of the experience. With each new project our archive of graphics continues to grow and our methodology continues to develop.

CONCLUSION

Our methodology is constantly evolving, as are many of our works, projects, and graphics. We often build upon past experiences to create our own deeper knowledge. We work to maintain our partnerships and collaborations, rather than produce one-off experiences. As a collective, we've created our own vernacular language and aesthetic, and as we grow and evolve we've begun to notice themes and styles that constantly pop up in our work and in collaborations with the public. This shared production grows, and much like our principals, it is not stagnant, and it is not final. It is an ongoing process of creating and building solidarity and unity—with the public, the groups we collaborate with, and amongst ourselves.

BRIDGET ELMER, JANELLE REBEL, MARSHALL WEBER

Freedom of the Presses

Activating Library Resources through Collaborative Curating

IN CONVERSATION
December 1, 2017

Freedom of the Presses was a collaborative, multi-site exhibition and event program at Ringling College of Art and Design that ran from October 20 to December 2, 2017. It was co-curated by Booklyn and members of the Ringling College community to focus on the creative and democratic processes of twenty-first-century independent artists' publishing, as well as models of empowering and educational art-publishing practices.

Janelle Rebel: You both worked on a curatorial missive for *Freedom of the Presses* early on, but how would you describe the show now, as it is soon closing?

Bridget Elmer: We wanted to showcase collaborative making and publication as social practice, and we also ended up modeling that process through curating, installing, experiencing the exhibit, and organizing the programming. I think that's a missing piece in the initial description of the show.

Marshall Weber: Booklyn's goal in the project was to help the institution activate its collections so I did spend a lot of time looking at work from Ringling College. This is one of those invisible elements that wasn't necessarily apparent in the show. I also found the curatorial process really interesting, in terms of how that process redefined the Ringling College collections to both Janelle as the librarian and to Bridget as a faculty member.

Bluebird Book Bus and NOMAD Art Bus, 2017, at the *Freedom of the Presses* book fair, Ringling College of Art and Design, Sarasota, FL. Photo: Rhonda Stapleton

Brian
Sophia

JR: For the exhibition at the [Richard and Barbara] Basch Gallery, half of the work came from Booklyn and half of it from the [Brizdle-Schoenberg] Special Collections Center. When we were exploring materials to include from Special Collections, was there a moment when the material focus of the show became clear to you?

BE: Our process of curating work from Special Collections did feel like a conversation with the work from Booklyn. Seeing the checklist from Booklyn helped us narrow what we initially pulled from our collection. That first pass through *was* nebulous. We intentionally left things open.

MW: Yes. I went into the show with this idea that I was *only* going to present collaborative work. I had a bracket that was pretty precise. But it wasn't my intention to have that bracket contain the whole show. There was this idea that the work from Booklyn would be a catalyst. The Booklyn material was really recent material, while we knew that the material from Ringling College would offer a more historical perspective.

JR: And actually when we started looking at our collections, we decided not to bring in a historical perspective but use the exhibition as an opportunity to acquire current material by other collaborative groups or artists working in a social practice mode. For me, everything clicked when we acquired *Beauty in Transition* by Jody Wood and Emily Larned. It added a different beat. Suddenly the work from both collections seemed to fall into alignment. We were working with a really diverse mix of projects and practices.

MW: In our conversations, one of the most interesting things that came up was this idea of a spectrum of processes that ranged from social commentary on one side (which can be really removed or even privileged) to social practice and collaborative work on the other side (which was either agit-prop or specific community and policy work).

JR: I've been curious about the decision to name the show *Freedom of the Presses*—a title that could mean so many different things. When I first heard it, I was thinking about the history of print censors and regulators, or of freedom of expression and journalism and our post-truth moment.

BE: The naming was early in the process, and for me it was really effective at pinpointing something that I wanted to bring to the fore in our campus consciousness, which is the idea that owning your own press is really the

IVAW portfolio installation, 2017, *Freedom of the Presses* exhibition, Brizdle-Schoenberg Special Collections Center, Ringling College of Art and Design, Sarasota, FL. Photo: Marshall Weber

only way to have the freedom of the press. It was important that the title be accessible. I didn't want to pin it down any further than that because it would get too granular.

MW: I imagined "freedom of the presses" to describe the release of the definition of an artists' book from the tyranny of both the fine press and conventional trade book. In the United States, when one thinks of the press, when one thinks of publishing, our roots are with printed dissent, the Declaration of Independence or Thomas Paine's *Common Sense*. Historical print culture in the U.S. is primarily associated with newspapers, and thus I thought also of the American obsession with the freedom of the press—this idea that you should be able to print whatever you want. I wanted the exhibition to celebrate this pragmatic, idealistic, and immediate sense of Pan-American culture. From there you get to freedom of expression, which is all about being able to print *how*ever you want to print. It's the kind of freedom of the presses where "comics are legit," "silkscreen is legit," "risograph is legit," "zines are legit," "graphic novels are legit."

VIVISECTIONARY
VIVISECTIONARY
INCISION
GIRLS AND THEIR FOOD ON INSTAGRAM VOLUME II
SOFIA SZAMOSI

JR: And in terms of freeing the artists' book, we attempted to echo those ideas in the installation of the exhibition. The Basch Gallery was part reading room, part exhibition space; and the Special Collections Center was turned into an immersive installation of the portfolio *Celebrate People's History: Iraq Veterans Against the War*. But I think even beyond this, the programming, which largely happened outside of the gallery, was really important.

BE: Originally what I imagined was the show, a curator's panel, an artist talk with Marshall, and a book fair that was very small in scale—modeled more on a zine fest. And then as the word spread that we were doing the show, that we were doing a book fair, all of these people came out of the woodwork with interest. The book fair took on its own sort of identity because of the expansion of collaborative partners on and off campus. The film screening fell into place because there was a group that had coalesced in St. Pete around social practice and they were already organizing these informational film screenings. We realized that some of those films featured artists in the show. I wanted to bring in some interactive, intergenerational projects that were easy to see and could bring people into the library and into the gallery. I ended up collaborating with some regional groups that focus on social practice. It kind of just kept ballooning, which was very affirming but also overwhelming.

MW: That's great. This is one of the primary issues about the idea of *Freedom of the Presses*. The idea of outreach is so crucial and the idea of having the gallery or Special Collections be an anchor for programming that reaches across campus and maybe, or even more importantly, into the local community. For me the ultimate goal is that these kind of shows should be the status quo instead of the exception.

JR: One of the projects that fostered a connection on campus and with the public was the *HaikU Road Signs* project. Exile Books worked in collaboration with Eleanor Eichenbaum, a faculty member here, to lead a poetry workshop with students and faculty. The collected haikus were then programmed on LED road signs and positioned throughout campus and on the main

Booklyn's zine table, *Freedom of the Presses Book Fair*, 2017, Alfred R. Goldstein Library, Ringling College of Art and Design, Sarasota, FL. Photo: Rhonda Stapleton

I Wish To Say, 2017, Sheryl Oring, performance, Alfred R. Goldstein Library, Ringling College of Art and Design, Sarasota, FL. Photo: Rhonda Stapleton

thoroughfare. We're so used to seeing construction-related visuals on campus, but these made you take a second look. I saw some sleep-deprived students stop in their tracks as the line "this is not a sign" scrolled by.

BE: The road signs are another example of programming that developed out of an initial idea for outreach that was pretty limited. Exile Books is doing great work down in Miami and I invited them to be at the book fair, along with Booklyn, to represent what's going on in a contemporary context. They sent me images of the *HaikU Road Signs* project and I just decided that we had to make it happen. It was not a part of the original lineup. But it was so exciting and it ended up pulling in faculty who had not been involved.

MW: I didn't get to participate in some of the programming like the zine fair or Sheryl Oring's performance. I'm wondering if you could both talk about her involvement.

BE: Sheryl was here as a visiting artist during the book fair. Her project, *I Wish to Say: Postcards to the President*, is a performative social-practice art piece that she's been engaging and activating since 2004. We got some background about her project through the film screening. She also presented an artist talk on campus. Then she performed during the book fair, taking dictation and typing postcards to the president during the fair. It was a really comprehensive and exciting experience. We had a lot of participation. People of all ilk stopped. There were students, there were faculty and staff, and there were also community members who participated.

Seeing the interest, and then also getting to read [the postcards]—I had the privilege to read everything that was dictated that day—it was so revealing, interesting, and appropriate to the mission of the show. We're going to publish some of what was collected that day. It will be a collaborative project with Sheryl that we address in our artist's publication course. We're also planning a documentary publication that will be produced in that class about *Freedom of the Presses*. It's very exciting. Sheryl's super excited to continue the engagement with our campus, which is great. What was your perception?

Installation view, 2017, *Freedom of the Presses* exhibition, Richard and Barbara Basch Gallery, Ringling College of Art and Design, Sarasota, FL. Photo: Nancy Nassiff

One of the *HaikU Road Signs* on the edge of campus during the Freedom of the Presses exhibition, 2017, Ringling College of Art and Design, Sarasota, FL. Photo: Bridget Elmer

JR: I queued up when she was here to dictate my postcard to the president. There's an inviting element of play that compels you to participate—her retro clerical appearance, red-white-and-blue graphics, and manual typewriter. Within the confines of that play structure, you get work done without it seeming like work. So it was a surprisingly pleasurable experience even though I was dictating a caustic letter to the president. And the conversations with students around Sheryl's typewriter stand made it especially worthwhile. One student said, "I have *so much* to say. How do I begin?"

BE: It was really important that she was there because of the way that her project clarified the mission of the show—in the same way that Jody Wood's book clarified the mission for you. The way that Sheryl's project is designed enacts this idea so simply, but there is also such complexity within it and activated by it — but you can process it in a minute or less. That was also really important to me—to have something happening that put social practice into motion.

We've talked a lot about how this show could be a kind of beta test for this model of an outside organization like Booklyn becoming a catalyst for a very regional, campus-specific experience. Marshall, are you imagining that you'll move this model to other places? Are there things that you will definitely do as we modeled them? Or other things that you would change, based on the experience?

MW: In part this show evidences Booklyn's current focus on collaborations with schools and social-justice organizations as sources of creative publishing. I feel that this entire experience made me want to move even further away from passive social commentary towards artists' books focused on active social practice and even direct political action. It sharpened my commitment to establish a more definitive pedagogy when working with schools at every level, from preschools to universities. It made me reconfirm Booklyn's goal of going beyond the distribution of work for activist artists and using that mechanism to support social-justice organizations, to form networks of artists, educators, and institutions. I think this show was instructive for further defining how to realize these intentions. So yes, we would like to see it happen at other institutions. I think the Ringling College show provides a good template for this. Staff and faculty were courageous in adopting that model and really tried to realize it fully. And I would love to see more academic libraries and galleries give that a try. I'm super excited and curious to see what follow-up publications you and your students and staff produce next.

BE: Me too. I am grateful to both of you for all of the work and risks that you took with me. I feel really excited about what we've modeled—both for our institution, because I hope to keep working in this way, interdepartmentally, and also what this potentially models on a larger scale. So thank you so much.

ANTON WÜRTH

The Use of Type in Artists' Books

Provided that type is part of the value system of civilization and provided that it is the task of art to question this value system, the use of type in artists' books is a reflection on the use of type by means of type.

WHY IS TYPE often scattered over the pages in an uncontrolled manner in artists' books? Or why are letters sometimes superimposed so that they become illegible? And why, in other instances, do we have to deal with fragments of "A"s and "O"s that are thus rendered only partially identifiable? What are we to make of all this? Are there specific reasons for each of these designs—or do they all share an underlying motive? Are we talking about a simple infringement of established rules or about outright innovation? I would like to explore these questions further, for I believe that one possible reason for arranging type in all these incomprehensible ways is implied by writing itself: it seems to me that what is challenged here is the function of writing as the representation of spoken language, which is based on the presumption that writing is equivalent to spoken language. A conceptual discussion of writing seems thus to be of the utmost importance since writing is not only the main focus of most artists' books but also serves equally as the taciturn cultural foundation of daily life.

1. THE CULTURAL IDEA OF TYPE

Within the occidental European model of civilization, a *historical mind* or *historical consciousness*, "the recording and remembering of events and persons as well as the telling of stories from the past,"[1] is closely linked to written records. This is not to say that societies without a culture of writing do not have a sense of history. It rather demonstrates the constitutive and structuring power attributed to written records in certain societies.[2] The written note coincides with the conception of a linearity of history as a continuous succession (Homer, *catena aurea*) in an effort to retrace one's origins to a first beginning and to legitimize power. As an establishing device the written note cannot be separated from the pretension to power and from its expansion. The genealogies of the Sumerian King List are early examples of this. But the Icelandic *Trójumanna saga* of the thirteenth century also follows the common practice of medieval texts, tracing the origins of those powerful rulers it refers to back to Troy. The formation of social institutions (administrative and legislative) is connected, too, with written records. Laws are registered and published. Since they are publicly accessible they are of constitutive validity. Further, written records played a crucial role in the establishment of an organized trade system. Inventories of merchandise are among the earliest written documents.

The invention of movable characters and letterpress printing of books represents a decisive step beyond the scripting of spoken words into handwritten language.[3] To this first step of transformation another is then added: the manual, as well as individualistic processing and spreading of information is now transformed into a mechanical, systematic, and unified act of communication through language in print. This transformative moment is the central theme of Marshall McLuhan's study, *The Gutenberg Galaxy*.[4] For McLuhan, the transition from the age of manuscript to that of the printing press marks a crucial cesura toward a more limited mode of perception. According to McLuhan, printed script is perceived predominantly visually to the detriment of all other senses. "For writing is a visual enclosure of non-visual spaces and senses."[5] This transformation involves the standardization of types and the automation of copying through print. At the same time, orthography and grammar dictate normative rules that set the sequential order for the expression of content and define the ways in which content appears in print. This process of standardization was initiated in Europe by Alkuin of York in the eighth century during the Carolingian Renaissance. Alkuin's reform of writing became the foundation for a unified system of writing all over Europe. This process of standardization also implies an accessibility of knowledge, a notion that is fundamentally democratic. At the same time, this development causes a stronger determinism and more segmentisation through analytical separations. We have reached the starting point of the institutionalization of type as well as that of its

Die Beete im Botanischen Garten sind nach Gattungen und Vegetationszonen angelegt. Neben manchen Pflanzen steht die Beschriftung noch auf alten Emailschildchen: wissenschaftliche Bezeichnung, Herkunftsland, Aufnahmejahr und Inventarnummer. Die Schrift auf dem Schild ist eingerahmt. Ich muss genau hinsehen. Der üppige Rahmen stört die Lesbarkeit erheblich. Die Besuchszeit geht zu Ende. Es wird auch dieses Mal wieder später werden. Die Ankunft ist für neunzehn Uhr geplant. Auf halbem Weg erinnere ich mich: Die Ruhe ist tatsächlich sichtbar. Sie ist eine Unterbrechung in der fortschreitenden Bewegung der Zeit, aber nicht regungslos. In der Anleitung für das Märchen ist das Ereignis nur Rohmaterial. Es steht als Stichwort auf dem Merkzettel und wird im richtigen Moment Losungswort.

Die Sequenz aus vier Fotos zeigt immer die gleiche Situation: Einer sitzt am Steuer und hält mit beiden Händen das Lenkrad fest. Der Beifahrer hat seinen linken Arm auf der Rückenlehne der durchgehenden Sitzbank ausgestreckt. Der Betrachter ändert das Gesehene. Er nimmt den Platz des Fotografen auf dem Rücksitz ein und richtet das Objektiv zwischen den beiden vor ihm Sitzenden durch die Windschutzscheibe auf die Straße. Die Schranke am Übergang ist noch geschlossen. Der Mittelstreifen teilt auch das Bild. 507

Lear: *(...) Hewgh! Give the word.*
Edgar: *Sweet marjoram.**
Lear: *Pass*[1]

* *Majoran wurde als Heilpflanze gegen Wahnsinn verwendet.*

1 William Shakespeare, König Lear, 4. Akt 6. Szene

Halbjahr, 1999, Anton Würth, artists' book. Photo: C.G. Boerner

Ich bin ganz in das Spiel vertieft. Ich schließe abwechselnd das linke und das rechte Auge und lasse dabei den ausgestreckten Daumen vor der Stuhllehne hin- und her- springen. Im Spiel, verstanden als die Abfolge ergebnisorientierter Funktionen, ist eine Abweichung von den Spielregeln nicht vorgesehen. „Die schönen Tage von Aranjuez sind nun zu Ende.“[2] *Wäre der Infant einen Tag länger geblieben... Der Blick auf das flache Land ist mit Häuserreihen verstellt. Die Häuserreihen sind wie Wassertriebe, die zurückgeschnitten werden müssten. Inzwischen wohnen andere hier. Die Mieter wechseln ständig. Noch bin ich unterwegs. Ich suche eine Landmarke und bestimme den gegenwärtigen Standpunkt auf der Karte. Die Kuppe ist unübersichtlich. Dahinter verläuft die Grenze. Ich zögere und vergewissere mich. Als bringe mich die Wiedererkennung näher heran. Die Richtung ist unverändert. 1758*

Die Sequenz aus vier Fotos zeigt immer die gleiche Situation: Einer sitzt am Steuer und hält mit beiden Händen das Lenkrad fest. Der Beifahrer hat seinen linken Arm auf der Rückenlehne der durchgehenden Sitzbank ausgestreckt. Der Betrachter ändert das Gesehene. Er nimmt den Platz des Fotografen auf dem Rücksitz ein und richtet das Objektiv zwischen den beiden vor ihm Sitzenden durch die Windschutzscheibe auf die Straße. Die Schranke am Übergang ist noch geschlossen. Der Mittelstreifen teilt auch das Bild. 507

2 Friedrich Schiller, Don Carlos, 1. Akt 1. Auftritt

carrier—the book, a situation that will inevitably lead to an unprecedented network of communication and will have a formative influence on Western civilization.[6] The cultural idea of type and of the book as its carrier effectively establishes society and shapes identity (the formation of nation-states and national languages). These processes were to a large extent completed within the first two hundred years following the invention of printing with movable type.[7]

To be part of a society one must be able to recognize its signs. Their meaning coins the imagination of reality and creates culture. The written mode mirrors a specific idea of reality. From this idea a conceptual continuum originates, along which the rational mind moves toward an increasingly conscious perception of reality. Our Western codification of a letter-writing system is likewise arranged according to a progressive linearity. This linearity is inseparable from the traditional concept of time as a continuous succession of coming into being and passing away that is inevitably experienced as progress. Our perception is coined accordingly. In response to this model of linearity an inventory of analytic concepts has been created on which our philosophical and scientific thinking is commonly based. Whereas during the manuscript culture of the Middle Ages *disputatio* and visual perception were the predominant means of gaining knowledge, recognition now shifts toward bookkeeping and the applied sciences. McLuhan talks about "light *through*" that now substitutes for "light *on*."[8] The norm of linearity determines the perspective of logocentric occidental thinking. It is connected with our understanding of history and with the Christian belief in creation and resurrection as well as with belief in progress represented by modernity. The ideas of writing and of the book as the container or carrier of writing or space for it *are both closely connected with the assumption of a linear understanding of the human condition.*

As storage space or container, writing is a material support of memory. At the same time, it also counts as a metaphor for remembrance. For Plato, writing is the reason for forgetfulness. He says that when one trusts the strange signs (writing), then the inner signs (independent thinking) are neglected. "For this invention [of written letters] will produce forgetfulness in the minds of those who learn to use it, because they will not practice their memory. Their trust in writing, produced by external characters which are no part of themselves, will discourage the use of their own memory within them. You have invented an elixir not of memory, but of reminding; and you offer your pupils the appearance of wisdom, not true wisdom."[9] While Plato criticizes the heteronomy of the written record, Aristotle says that "Spoken words are the symbols of mental experience and written words are the symbols of spoken words."[10] Horace invokes the durability of writing in an ode in which he compares writing to a monument: "*Exegi monumentum aere perennius*" (I have made a monument more lasting than bronze).[11] Expressing his conviction that writing guarantees durability while even monuments cast in bronze will not last forever, Horace pays homage to the myth of the permanence of a text fixed in writing, whereas the orally transmitted text is considered to be less truthful.[12] Two thousand years later, Friedrich Hegel asserts the primacy of the written text in his *Encyclopedia*, arguing that it is the most intelligent way of writing, and Jean-Jacques Rousseau observes in his *Essay on the Origin of Language* that, in contrast to writing with syllables or pictures (habits that according to him belong to the world of barbarians and savages), writing with letters is an indication of civilization. Writing is seen by these philosophers as a medium that most immediately represents thinking. It is presented as equivalent to the mind itself, especially since in the course of reading, letters lose their materiality and vanish, becoming transparent carriers of thought. Since the Renaissance and its discourse about the competition between written and pictorial representation, writing has been associated with the rationality of logos and science; through this association between writing and scientific accuracy the use of type lays claim to the representation of truth itself. "These metaphysics of writing, originating from the Renaissance, remain present in certain contexts to this day."[13]

Although "writing and the drawn line are equally graphic, and although writing and drawing are in correlation due to their pictorial quality,"[14] we retain the traditional distinction between writing and drawing. This is especially true for the book. An image counts as mimetically biased while a word is considered to be abstract. Images are multidimensional and not suited to conveying exact descriptions. But text and image also are in a dialectic relationship. While texts interpret images, images illustrate texts. "We argue that before the invention of letterpress printing, the dialectic text/image was the elastic spring that drove Western history."[15]

After this introductory approach to the cultural phenomenon of *type*, I would like to emphasize the complexity of the simple word "*use*" in this essay's title. I will give a short summary of the character of type and then go on to explain how type functions as *sign*. My understanding is guided by both theoretical and practical aspects: practical use (application) is as important as theoretical examination (idea). Both must be acknowledged because both have an essential impact on creative decisions. Within the context of my investigation the *book* functions as a space of reference where type is imprinted. The book is the carrier of type. It fulfills the function of an archive and is a medium of communication of information coded in type. The particular formal and cultural quality of the book has a decisive impact on the use and the perception of type. The context in which type is perceived is crucial for its impact on meaning. It makes a difference whether writing is chiseled in stone on a monument, handwritten on a scroll, or printed in a book. I would like to define *art* as a technique of reflection that combines theory and craft, *mind and matter*. Through this means art launches its *critique*. I understand *critique* as the exploration of the circumstances of a given problem and as the verification of its conditions.

Book art for me, therefore, represents a reflection on the conditions and functional potentials of the book. In book art, the book becomes the subject of artistic expression—a self-referential medium "that not only represents reality but that also presents itself as reality."[16] The book is taken over by artistic freedom and the reader becomes part of a discourse that forces him to act and to judge. From this results the task of "clearing out the clearing,"[17] in which the book is situated due to its form and contents as a cultural idea. Given our specific perspective, this clearing (Heidegger literally talks about *lichten des Spielraums* = clearing/lightening the space to play) must recognize the following problems:

- How does the visual expression of language-coded (i.e. spoken) information function with the help of printed type (i.e. in writing) when we consider above all its mediating codification in the book?
- What effect does the writing in letters have on our perception? Is the artists' book a possible locus for an examination of this problem?
- What does "artistic expression" have to contribute to an examination of a reflected use of type?

2. WRITING, TYPE (THE ALPHABET)

"Writing is language written up."[18] "Writing equals the quantity of graphic signs needed to record spoken language."[19] "Writing in its true meaning is present when two assumptions are fulfilled: First: A graphic activity (painting, drawing, scratching, printing) must occur. Second: Communication should be successfully established—either with others in an exchange of information or with oneself as a memory aid."[20] In the former case, writing functions as medium, and in the latter as means. Writing records spoken language. Writing communicates language. Writing mediates language independently from the presence of the author. The phenomenon *type* is supported by the framework of language. Through writing, language is textualized. The ephemeral phenomenon of spoken language is fixed as text and thus in its written form language gains an independent *Gestalt* (shape and form). Written language becomes independent of spoken language. This is what we refer to when we talk of *language determined by type*.

A remark from the dictionary. In English the word "type" *refers to writing in print. The word* "writing" *stands for all forms of visual representation of language in general. German has a single word*—"Schrift"—*for both type and (hand)writing. The distinction between the printed or written status of the text is marked by an adjective or determined by the context. I would like to stress the importance of making clear distinctions between language that is spoken, handwritten, or printed.*

Writing consists of a limited inventory of signs—*the alphabet*. "Basically any of the lists of letters or characters used by different languages to compose all their words could be referred to as *alphabet*."[21] Our writing system is a set of phonetic letters. "It relates to the colloquial language as its message."[22] A single sound in spoken language carries no meaning. In the written language system each sound of spoken language is referred to by a specific visual sign (type-sign). By common agreement, every sound has an equivalent in a sign. This convention guarantees recognition and readability. We call this agreement "codification." Codification guarantees that every specific sound of the spoken language is assigned to a certain visual sign of the alphabet called a letter. Our writing is codified in an alphanumeric fashion with both letters and numbers. This kind of writing is intended to guarantee the fixation of spoken words with the help of graphic signs and to express the written transmission of spoken language. It would apply equally to refer to *writing as determined by language* in this context. The decoding of the visual sign is called *reading*. Reading is the comprehensive perception of writing as language. The system that structures language in comprehensible connections is called grammar. The system that arranges type as readable text on the type carrier is called typography.

A system of notation is a system of signs that is free of ambiguities and allows for syntactic and semantic disjunction (no two characters share an object of application) as well as for differentiation (thus disjunction is effective). Roughly speaking a maximum of syntactic and semantic unambiguity[33] is realized in such a system."

Writing and type are systems of notation linked by two aspects:

1. The visual sign: grapheme

A letter is the smallest unit (*grapheme*) of our written Western language codification, the *alphabet*. Each single letter is a visual event: it has a form and a dimension, an expansiveness. It is related to space and possesses a physical shape, a *Gestalt.* The letter is generated through a process of abstraction from images. The process of abstraction involves several stages: From the (multidimensional) image to pictorial writing (still present in traffic signs, for example) to (one-dimensional) letter writing. The history of writing provides detailed information about the characters from *capitalis quadrata* to computer-generated screen characters.

A letter/character is the smallest unit of writing. One letter rarely appears alone. The single letter, taken on its own, has no meaning. It receives its meaning through the connection to and in the context of other letters. We call this association with others "writing," "type," or "text." Writing groups single letters into words (type setting) and terms. The words are combined to create sentences according to the rules of grammar. The sentences are lined up one after the other in rows along lines in progression from top to bottom and from left to right. Writing is on-line. Writing is related to the concept of time as a continuous process of succession. Writing is determined by progressive linearity. I shall continue to refer to this way of orientation of writing as *the linear sequence* or *the linearity of writing.*

2. The acoustic sign: phoneme

The shape of the letter represents a linguistic sound. The letter marks a sound notation, *the phoneme*. The phoneme is the smallest unit in language to carry distinct meaning. Phonemes distinguish between words in so-called *minimal pairs*. For example, "house" and "hose" differ by one vowel phoneme; "good" and "hood" by one consonant phoneme. The shape of a letter is assigned to a phoneme. But a phoneme does not automatically correspond to a single grapheme. There can also be combined graphemes like "th." Graphically identical signs can be realized in different ways in spoken language depending on pronunciation. The different acoustic realizations of the same letter are called *phones*. A phone is a sound unit, too, but has no distinguishing function; it is an accent.

In its appearances as grapheme as well as phoneme, the letter stands vicariously as a sign for a specific meaning. Each letter has a quality of content—its signification—and a quality of form—its visual appearance. "By the meaningless sign linked to the meaningless sound we have built the shape and meaning of Western man."[24] Talking about type means talking about *mind and matter*. In the case of *mind* (content, information, aim of communication) we face the problem of representation of meaning by means of type, i.e. of language signs, which takes us into *semiotics*. Talking about *matter* (graphic activity, envisioning information, practical use) we face the problem of form and its layout in space, here: on the double spread of the book page, which opens our perspective towards *typography*. I will discuss the use of type in artists' books under these two aspects: theory (semiotics) and practical application/use (typography).

3. SEMIOTICS (CONCEPTUALIZING TYPE)

"Language and writing are two different systems of signs; the purpose of the latter is exclusively to represent the former."[25] Thus *sign* always refers to something that is not the sign itself.[26] The status of representation is essentially linked to the idea of the sign. In our context, a spoken word is represented (mediated, substituted, replaced) by a printed type—sign. The representational function of the (type-)sign plays a central role in any semiotic consideration.

According to *the structuralist conception of semiotics*, signs function in a binary way. A sign carrier (*signifier*, the denominating) is assigned to a denotation (*signified*, the denominated). The denominating *signifier*, an imagination, for example, is materialized by its carrier—*the signified.* The connection between signified and signifier constitutes the sign. In the context of writing, one can say that a term (an imagination)/the signifier is embodied by the type/the signified. Together they build the (type-)sign, for example the (letter-)sign *A* or the (term-)sign *tree.* The (type-)sign is then assigned to an object. The (term-)sign *tree* gets assigned to a plant with trunk, branches, and leaves.

Thus the sign deals with two relationships:

a) an *internal relationship* between signifier and signified within the sign, which is constitutive to it;
b) an *external relationship* between the sign and its object, which constitutes reference i.e. meaning.

ANTON WÖRTH DEL. ET SCULP 2012
inferior superior
minor maior
prior posterior
exterior interior
debilior fortior
deterior peior
laetior tristior

Robert Nanteuil – Predella III, 2012, Anton Würth (appropriating Robert Nanteuil), artists' book. Photo: C.G. Boerner

Both relationships are grounded in representation. The idea of re-presentation, of making present what is not, but also of substituting or replacing something with something different (an object with a term) is based on the principle of assignment and not on an assumption of similarity. Assignment has to occur for the sake of a successful representation. The understanding of representation as substitution is based on analytic reasoning[27] and tries to prescribe that representation is successful. This success of representation is a claim on which our daily acts of communication rely heavily in order to function smoothly.

The unity of form and content in a sign is guaranteed as long as signified and signifier are supposed to be identical and the assignment of object and term is agreed upon unequivocally. I consider a book that reproduces such assignments without reflecting upon them as a stable entity.

a1) As (type-)sign, the sign becomes the medium in which the fugitive acoustic signals of the spoken word are stored. As a technical medium of notation, the type-sign is considered to achieve representation and to record spoken language without any losses of meaning. During this process of scripting, a transfer from the audible medium of *speaking* into the visual medium of *writing* occurs. That means that the type-sign as a graphic figure (the letter as form) is identified with its content (the language term). It is taken for granted that during this transfer no losses of meaning occur—a conceptualization that is mono-causal and insists on a symmetry between acoustic and visual signs. I suggest that we refer to this as a *semiotic understanding of the linearity of writing.*

a2) Since every transmission of spoken language as written language aims to have a certain effect and expresses a subjective point of view, we must not skip over the problem that codification implies mediation. I consider the assumption that representation is linear and objective as one that is obsolete. In any kind of transmission there is an involuntary loss so that difference gapes where unity is claimed. Since even the difference between written and spoken words cannot be fully bridged, any notion of adequate representation is doomed to fail. It is important to be aware of this failure of representation. Spoken language is forced into writing and restrained within the corset of its rationality.

b1) The nature of the sign is referential. It refers to something that in itself is not a sign. The sign is in a relationship of reference to that which it stands for as sign. This referential quality of the sign is considered to operate in an immediate and linear manner and implies that the sign successfully represents the object it refers to. Thus it is by common agreement that meaning is assigned to a sign. Its readability is based on this agreement.

b2) The assertion that representation could be successful fails to acknowledge that every reference implies a loss of or a shift in meaning and, therefore, maintains the separateness of form and content. Reference is substitution, a sign is a replacement that perpetuates rather than overcomes the dis-similarity of form and content. The representation of the original is no longer the original. Reference to the origin is not original. The desire for a re-presentation, which makes the original present, must remain unfulfilled. The sign, therefore, marks the difference or dis-similarity between itself and the object. Therefore, I consider it more credible to ponder the disparity of transmission than to base my thoughts on an assertion of unity. I would like to replace *unity* with *difference*.

4. TYPOGRAPHY (DEMATERIALIZATION OF TYPE)

In the context of my reflection on the use of type in artists' books, I must add yet another component to the process of the scripting of spoken words into writing, one that goes beyond the previously mentioned semiotic aspects of writing: typography, which arranges the written words to be printed. Marshall McLuhan recognizes its importance when he subtitles his *Gutenberg Galaxy* with "The Making of Typographic Man." The single type, in its formal use as a graphic sign, serves as a means of expression. The creative decisions in its application, however, are not influenced by the arguments gleaned from semiotics. From the point of typography, type is a mere stepping-stone. Here, formal and functional aspects of design and layout take precedence. Unlike semiotics, typography does not challenge the unity of form and content in the sign. In this context, the meaning of a sign is taken as a given.

"Letters of the alphabet that are cast or founded for the purpose of impressing upon paper are known as 'types' and the impression thus made as a 'print.'"[28] The words *to print* suggest that something leaves its imprint, thus implying a process of transmission. As a matter of fact, printing involves the transmission of a matrix or prototype from a stencil, model, or stamp to a new medium of paper or metal. In this way, printing not only creates a copy but also allows for the multiplication of an original.

Once this original is created, typography translates pictorial and textual information into a matrix to be imprinted on the pages of books.

Type, the printed letter, expresses a measure of rational distance. Type is distinguished from the casual handwritten note by creative agency. Typography is (or at least should be) the conscious practical use of the type. Typography arranges and structures text and derives its meaning from the complex task of processing text and translating it from a manuscript into an intentional and consciously designed layout, as, for example, on the pages of a book. The most important principle of typographic design is the articulated order. Typography is based on distinction and connection as well as on the interplay of merging and separation. Through the means and according to the rules of typography, written information is visualized. The matching type face must be chosen according to the text. The page format guides the proportion of type and its relationship to space. In our case, the space of reference for typography is the double-page spread. The space is flat and rectangular with upper and lower margins and folded in the middle. The decisions of design concern margins and fold. The middle fold is of particular importance as an axis of symmetry. A distinction between right and left sides is established. This relation to space coincides with a relation to time. In 1925 Jan Tschichold published his *Elementare Typographie* as a special issue of the Bauhaus journal *Typographische Mitteilungen*. His first three axioms read as follows:

1. Typography stresses purpose.
2. The purpose of typography is communication (typography is a means of communication). The information has to appear in the most condensed, simplest, and most forceful way.
3. In order to make typography subservient to social purposes, both internal (i.e. content arranging) and external (i.e. various typographic means relating to each other) organizations of the materials used are necessary.

The British typographer and typographic theoretician Stanley Morison calls typography "the efficient means to an essentially utilitarian and only accidentally aesthetic end" and goes on to say that typography of books "requires an obedience to convention which is almost absolute."[29] According to Morison, book typography is functionally adequate as long as it is readable, pleasing to the eye, and inconspicuous—in other words, as long as type is dematerialized and rendered invisible as a carrier of information. The typographer must solve the problem of how to arrange the written information on the carrier to achieve a readable context and a smooth transmission of information. The criteria on which his decisions are based are issues of pure practicality. In his design the typographer is guided by formal criteria that apply to the function of a text and facilitate its *consumption*. A certain style is created according to the text. Style is in service. The reading direction determines a temporal sequence. The organization of a train of thought along lines of type complies with this temporal sequence.

This strictly formal and functional use of the type describes the requirements typography must meet. Thus type is relegated to a merely subservient status, with the transmission of information as its sole purpose. This kind of typography has been successful since it is efficient for the mediation of information and has become synonymous with the everyday use of type. In the course of the centuries, rules for and means of typography have become standardized. Despite changes in style, typography consistently follows a rigid line system and a fixed direction of reading. *I would like to characterize this as the practical meaning of linearity of the use of type.*

Regarding the standardization of type in its practical use and as a means of representing language, the *topos* of overcoming linearity recurs frequently in the scholarly literature. "Linearity is the displacement of a multidimensional symbolic thinking,"[30] wrote Jacques Derrida in his *Grammatology*. This also affects our perception, narrowing its scope. Linearity causes a reduction of diversity and creativity since, according to McLuhan, "single-plane lineal, visual, and sequential codification of experience is quite conventional and limited . . . It was not until the experience of mass production of exactly uniform and repeatable type, that the fission of the senses occurred, and the visual dimension broke away from the other senses."[31] He further observes "the ingraining of lineal, sequential habits, and the visual homogenizing of experience in print culture, and the relegation of auditory and other sensuous complexity to the background . . . However, this type of reduction or distortion of all experience to the scale of one sense only is in tendency the effect of typography on the arts and sciences as well as upon human sensibility."[32] In response to this I believe that the main impetus for the use of type in book art has to go in the opposite direction. Type in artists' books should leave reduction and standardization behind and instead promote a more integral, visual-tactile perception.

5. THE USE OF TYPE IN ARTISTS' BOOKS (MATERIALIZATION OF TYPE)

The use of type appears to be a common denominator. Type is a means of everyday communication. It is not perceived as something extraordinary. No one cares about type. It is not questioned. It is a given. And once you have learned reading and writing it simply works. The artists' book can serve as locus for a reflected, probing use of type. The idea of the book as an art form does not intend to substitute that of the functional role of the book but it coexists with it as a locus of dissent, one that allows an examination of what I have described as a stable entity, i.e. the standardized use of the type and the linear representation of language through type. The artist is required to continuously *reformulate his creative viewpoint to engage ceaselessly in dynamic interaction with the existing conventions in his surroundings.* It is typical for the book as an art form that it does not represent a given content in the affirmative. It is not bound by recognizable forms of standardization. The artists' book can serve as a critical medium of reflection upon formal elements as well as upon matters of content.

Perception is not a mere reception of reality which happens to somebody. Perception embraces a dialogue about our relation to reality and includes experience and action. This relationship is expressed through written notes and at the same time writing acts upon us as reality.

The model of configuration, type as subject

When the constrictions of mono-causality are abandoned, type itself can become subject to examination and is transformed into a topic. This approach opens a perspective of questioning and reflection on the use of type. The standardized corset of type is opened aesthetically. Design decisions are guided by a synthetic joining motion that counteracts rational analysis. A structural conception of text as texture is characteristic of the spatial extension (*Verräumlichung*) of language. The model of configuration widens the scope, something that already becomes obvious in the composition of the text. Mallarmé's "A Throw of the Dice" ("Un coup de dés jamais n'abolira le hasard", written in 1897) is the classic example of this. A paratactic coexistence and extension together substitute the succession that always aims for conclusion or, in a religious understanding, redemption.

The demand for a materialization of writing seeks to abolish its subservient status and to allow it to step forth as a medium in its own right.

In order to make writing perceptible, to expose it, to let it take effect and to give it conscious recognition, its special quality as a hybrid of language and image must be stressed. In botanical science, the hybrid denotes the result of cross breeding; the literal meaning of the word is "of dual origin." As a system of signs, writing has a pictorial quality. Like images, writing moves in a two-dimensional space. Writing occurs as a graphic manifestation on the face of the book page. Writing is visually perceptible. When we refer to the appearance of type or writing this becomes obvious. However, this fact is not usually examined further. On the other hand, writing is a standardized carrier of meaning and as a representative of language fades into the background. During the process of reading, writing as the transparent carrier of language does not appear as a separate entity. This is what I described as the dematerialization of writing. On the one hand, writing is a sign as others, a marker in the space, punctuation. On the other hand, writing is exposed as a system of signs that through their standardized character stand against other signs as carriers of meaning of language. Writing oscillates between language and image. As in a puzzle picture, sometimes its language-bound character stands out while at others its pictorial character comes to the fore. Sybille Krämer describes this oscillation between language and image as an "intermedial phenomenon."[33]

In my reflection on aspects of semiotics and typography, I have observed two manifestations of the model of the linear representation of writing: I have juxtaposed a highly conceptual framework with an extremely functional view. This polarization comprises the range of problems implied by the use of type. Semiotics is a theoretical approach based on the (type-)sign. Typography refers to the function of type in the context of its day-to-day use. The linear model of representation is based on the assumption that in the scripting of spoken/colloquial language the (type-)sign or letter corresponds to an (also phonetic) unity of form and content and that the analytic denotation of term to object is unambiguous. I maintain that this model can only fail as it is neither capable of solving the problem of distortions or loss of meaning that occur during shifts of media nor can it overcome the restrictive limitations of expression implied by a rigid system of order in which meaning must be fully integrated. The phonetic assumption of writing based on the assignment of a type sign to a sound of spoken language is standardized. The line system by which writing is bound is also standardized. Both constitute the formal frame of the text. Representation is based on standardizations that rely entirely on the functionality of the system of information. By common agreement its success is assumed.

The question is how to overcome (and not how to replace) this dogma of linearity, one that promotes a limited perception and remains deficient as a form of representation. The assumption of representation of language through writing without any loss or distortion is obsolete. Plato had already recognized this deficiency. In his *Phaidros* he counted letters among the figments of imagination and called them "external hulls."[34] He considered them inadequate to the task of fulfilling their own claim to be mediators of truth, a condition that might only occur, if at all, through immediate dialogue.

One has to use the creative quality of writing. The one-dimensional assumption that writing comprises a linear sequential order fails to recognize that writing makes use of space on the face of a book page. Thus, multidimensionality and simultaneity are inherent qualities of writing, elements that tend to be overlooked or too little recognized as long as writing is merely given a subservient status as representation of language. I maintain that book art should aim to overcome this limitation and reduction.

How can it work? How can this be imagined?

I consider the distinction of form and medium that the sociologist Niklas Luhmann postulates in his book *Die Kunst der Gesellschaft* (The Art of Society) as the basis of a model that allows us to conceptualize the use of the type in artists' books. I maintain that writing must be emphasized as a medium rather than being allowed to recede into its form—that of the text.[35]

The written text is the form. Writing is the medium. The form is accidental, as Luhmann writes, and does not express the nature of the medium. Thus, text does not express the nature of writing. It expresses information by binding it to a written form: the novel, the poem, the description. Text does not refer to writing. It refers to the content of the language which is mediated through writing. The form (i.e. the text), therefore, appears more accomplished than the medium (i.e. writing) and the medium fades into the form (hence the transparency of writing when reading a text). The medium consists of loose couplings of elements. "Loose" means an open majority of potential connections, observes Luhmann. The elements of our medium writing are letters or types. These letters or types combine to form open, unlimited—loose, that is—couplings of words that then amount to a text. When writing is acknowledged as the creative medium behind its form, the text, the emphasis shifts to the inherent potential of writing to visualize aspects of content that do not have to correspond with the acoustic level of spoken language.[36] For example, abbreviations do not correspond to spoken language. Footnotes and marginal notes create inter-textual connections while they are at the same time connected to writing as special markers. Their text parallels the linear flow of the main text, thus introducing an element of retardation. Writing understood as independent from spoken language can come to the fore as a medium in its own right, one that is more than a system of notation of spoken language.

1. The reference

The reference of writing changes once it is understood as independent from the immediate representation of language. The meaning of signs is not exclusively dictated by their representational valence but is equally defined by their spatial relationship to each other. The valence of the sign is not defined only by its status, i.e. "C" as the third letter of the alphabet, but also by its position as a marker within a larger composition. The distinction between the representational valence of a sign and its status accounts for the difference between text and texture.

2. Structure, the structure of meaning, construction/super structure, the inner formation

The structuralist approach in which text is understood as texture, points toward the significance of constellation. The particular structural feature of writing is its *interstice.* Writing is composed discretely: letters keep their distance from each other. They do not overlap. Within our system of writing, the *ligature* represents the most radical *rapprochement.* On the other hand, the distance between letters must not become too wide in order to avoid a loss of context with neighboring letters. Blanks and gaps between letters and words play an important role within the system of writing. They define the coordination of the types to each other; ultimately, blanks and gaps are responsible for the readability of the text.

In reference to typography, *micro-typography* describes the interstice as it affects word and line spacings, as well as the actual design of the letters. *Macro-typography* addresses interstice in the overarching context of the entire text amount, which is to be organized in reference to the type carrier of the page. Macro-typography deals with the layout of a text as a whole, with the relationship between headlines and body text. As mediums of interpretation of text, however, both micro-typography and macro-typography remain tied to form. To emphasize the independent nature of type, micro- and macro-typography must gain momentum in reference to content.

To achieve this objective, the meaning of a sign must also be defined by its location within the structure, by its status and its position, and by the place assigned to it within the book space. Therefore, the static *Gestalt* of the sign itself, which is tied to the idea of an inherent unity of representation, is replaced by dynamic relationships between signs (*Gestalten*) and their position to each other, which are available for free association. Through changes of the interstice these relationships can be redefined regardless of their reference to content. In this new context the valence of the (type-)sign also changes.

The sign is no longer defined exclusively by its function as a carrier of meaning and in reference to acoustic signals of spoken language. Type moves away from its status as subservient medium, acknowledged only as form, and becomes the medium that determines the configuration. In this way, type stresses its corporeality/spaciality and transcends one-dimensionality. In reference to its own corporeality, type has an expressive potential that lies beyond the context of spoken language. Thus type becomes available to free composition and opens new means of interpretation.

3. Performance (linguistical: the use of language), application in a specific situation, for a specific purpose

In a figurative sense, the blanks stand in for the gaps, which are ripped open by the failure of representation. The loss of and the shift in meaning that occur during the transmission of spoken language into writing leave a gap. This gap—struck through representation and not bridgeable through aesthetics—becomes a possible driving force of artistic expression. Of course, this driving force can only unfold if the gap is acknowledged as an object worthy of reflection and careful examination. In artists' books the failure of representation is recognized and is taken up as a subject through aesthetic means. The gap—in a formal as well as a figurative understanding—is a locus of interpretation, ambiguity, risk, and of creative openness. *The nature of writing lies in its blanks. The foundation for the symbolic implications of multidimensionality must be found in the gaps.* Any attempt at bringing closure to the gap opened by the failure of representation remains utopian. The acknowledgement that the gap cannot be bridged transforms failure into impulse. Hölderlin refers to such artistic effort as a "futile approach."[37] Any remark remains on the level of a pending possibility.

To begin to think of writing as independent of its ties to language requires a new approach to reading itself. In artists' books one cannot rely on a standardized—linear—development. The reader is included. He is no longer a mere consumer but must become actively involved. He has an option to be in dialogue to recreate the relationships outlined in the book and to make his own connections. His routine as reader is broken when the customary functionality of text is abandoned: condensation, leaping, rupture, fallowness must be overcome and brought into the context of space and content. This, too, lies in the nature of multidimensionality.

6. MY BOOKS

In my own work, I try to bring the various aspects discussed in the previous chapter together in an organized form I call the *Ornamental Principle*.[38] My aim is to combine text and image as equally valid parts within the double spread of a book. This coincides with a change of the organization of space and time within the composition of a book. While I maintain the successive "reading" of the book (i.e. the paging through the codex), I introduce both cyclical and simultaneous movements into the reception process. Time is reevaluated in its continuity. Its linear aspect means progress, development, continuation of a storyline and causal connection to what came before (*catena aurea*). The simultaneous aspect of configuration refers to its expansion within a two-dimensional plane, its duration, and its cyclical return (like the seasons in nature). I attempt to stage a ritualistic repetition of punctuation that helps to structure space within the pages of a book without providing a specific meaning.[39] "Every repetition implies the alteration of what is repeated as a structural possibility."[40] From this point onward the narrative aspect of a book changes. Its narrative is no longer necessarily tied to a storyline. Its structure confronts the narrative illustration. The principle of a chronological storytelling, of a linear plot, is substituted by the model of expansion, by the weaving together of the individual parts, creating the possibility of jumping in from different angles, of anticipating as well as reverting.

The subject of my book projects, therefore, is to plug the deficit inherent in all referential relations. This "deficit" is based on firm attributions that cannot ultimately be fulfilled. The system of writing, the text, exists only in its referential relationship to other elements. It depends on a clear denotation (meaning), homogenization (alphabet, grammar, syntax, spelling), and segmentation (division into such separate actions as typesetting and printing). This entails, as discussed above, a limitation of perception that leads to a deficit. I see ornament as a possible escape route from such limitation.

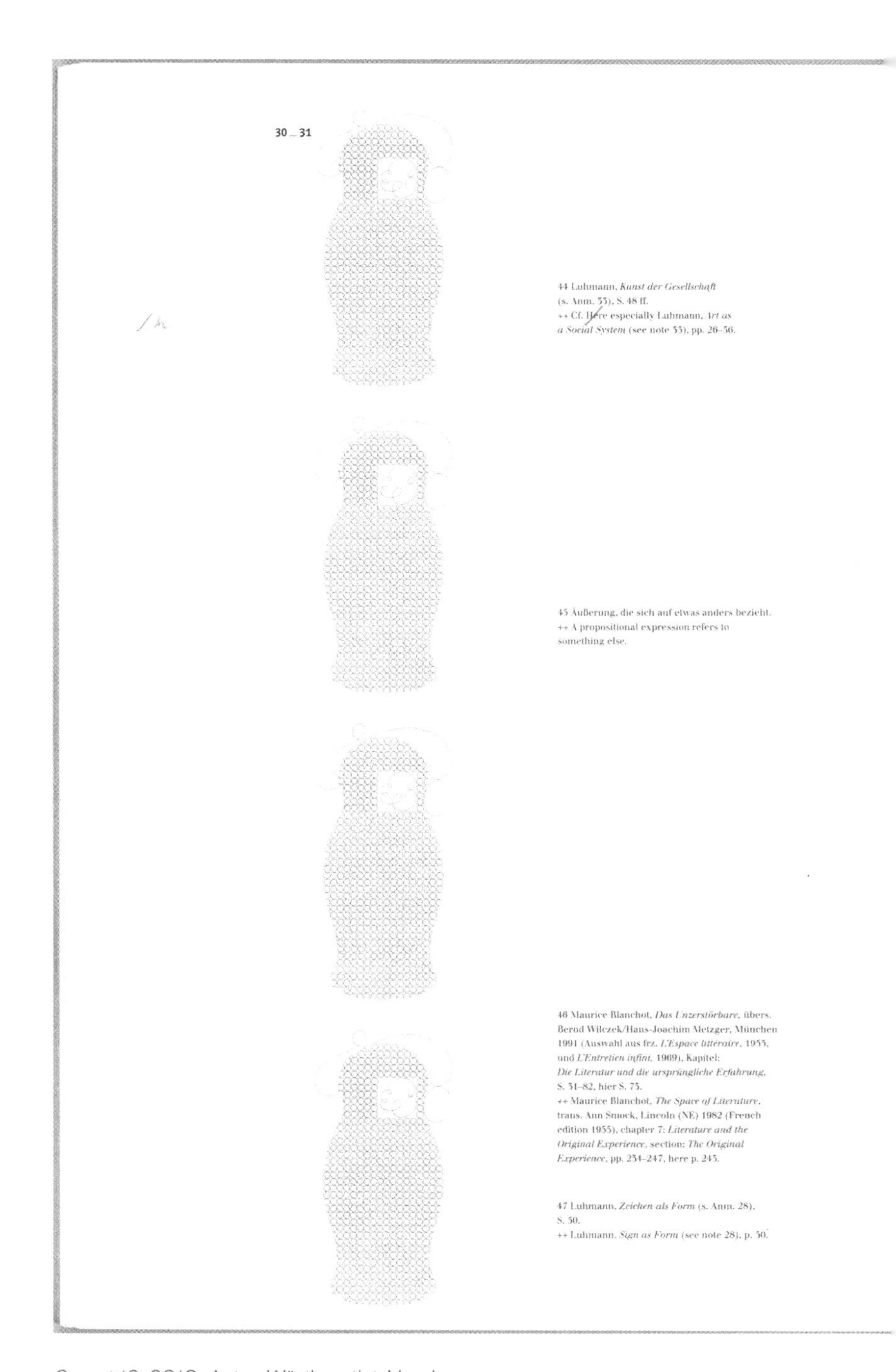

30_31

44 Luhmann, *Kunst der Gesellschaft* (s. Anm. 33), S. 48 ff.
++ Cf. Here especially Luhmann, *Art as a Social System* (see note 33), pp. 26–36.

45 Äußerung, die sich auf etwas anders bezieht.
++ A propositional expression refers to something else.

46 Maurice Blanchot, *Das Unzerstörbare*, übers. Bernd Wilczek/Hans-Joachim Metzger, München 1991 (Auswahl aus frz. *L'Espace littéraire*, 1955, und *L'Entretien infini*, 1969), Kapitel: *Die Literatur und die ursprüngliche Erfahrung*, S. 51–82, hier S. 73.
++ Maurice Blanchot, *The Space of Literature*, trans. Ann Smock, Lincoln (NE) 1982 (French edition 1955), chapter 7: *Literature and the Original Experience*, section: *The Original Experience*, pp. 234–247, here p. 243.

47 Luhmann, *Zeichen als Form* (s. Anm. 28), S. 50.
++ Luhmann, *Sign as Form* (see note 28), p. 50.

Carnet 16, 2010, Anton Würth, artists' book.
Photo: C.G. Boerner

Erweiterungsfunktion. +++ Das Ornament vereint/verkörpert/visualisiert sich als Differenz/Unterscheidung/Trennung und löst sich somit vom Objektbezug. +++ Um das Ornament jenseits seines Objektbezugs und als Ort des Geschehens zu beschreiben, muss der Formbegriff, verstanden als geordneter Zusammenhang von Elementen, von der Gestalt gelöst werden. Ich denke dann das Ornament nicht mehr als Verzierungselement, sondern als prozessualen Begriff. Um den prozessualen Aspekt zu fassen, ist eine Neubewertung der Begriffe Ornament und ornamental notwendig. +++ Im Folgenden ist mir dazu die Systemtheorie Niklas Luhmanns[44] Leitfaden. Angelehnt an seine Begrifflichkeit, die er mit soziologischem Bezug entwickelt, versuche ich meine Überlegungen des ornamentalen Gestaltens begrifflich zu fassen.

Das Ornament als Zeichen ohne Referenz

Das Ornament hat zunächst alle Eigenschaften eines Zeichens. Wenn man sich auf den zeichentheoretischen Ansatz bezieht, der Zeichen daran misst, dass sie auf etwas anderes verweisen, dann verweist es auf Etwas, das auch etwas anderes sein kann, auch wenn dieses Etwas als Nichts bezeichnet wird. Das Ornament als Zeichen visualisiert und transportiert eben die Information, dass es keine gibt. Ich bezeichne deshalb das Ornament als ein Zeichen ohne Referenz, weil es keine vorgegebene Bedeutung reproduziert und nichts Gegebenes repräsentiert. Der Philosoph Josef Simon bemerkt dazu, dass das Zeichen nichts über das Bezeichnete aussagt. Das Ornament ist weder semantisch noch mimetisch. Es ist keine propositionale Äußerung,[45] sondern ist unmittelbar. Es lebt als Raummarkierung durch strukturelle Bezüge, die Unterscheidungen markieren und nur sich selbst verpflichtet sind. Es strukturiert den Raum, ohne ihm Bedeutung zu geben. Das Ornament wird selbst zum Ort des Geschehens und rückt so seine Unmittelbarkeit ins Blickfeld der Aufmerksamkeit. +++ Wie jede künstlerische Äußerung, kommuniziert das Ornament jenseits des herkömmlichen Sprachgebrauchs. Es kommuniziert nicht mittelbar durch die Zuschreibung von Begriffen, die analytisches Verständnis erfordern, sondern unmittelbar, indem es eine Atmosphäre schafft, die über Konnotation ästhetisch symbolisches Verstehen hervorruft. +++ Mittelbarkeit ist Kennzeichen linearen Denkens und durch feste Vereinbarungen bestimmt. Am Ort der festen Vereinbarungen herrschen stabile Verhältnisse. Den Ort der stabilen Verhältnisse bezeichne ich als Mitte. Hier steht alles still. Stillstand besteht am Ort der stabilen Verhältnisse insofern, als die Einheit von Form und Inhalt, die Eineindeutigkeit der Repräsentation als gegeben vorausgesetzt wird. Daraus geht das Stillstehen als ein Resultat von Anfang und Ende hervor und bewegt sich in der Zeit. Dagegen bedeutet Stillstehen bezüglich der Unmittelbarkeit Affirmation. „Diese Bejahung ist die Fortdauer dessen, was weder Beginn noch Ende erträgt, der Stillstand, der weder erschafft noch zerstört, was niemals hergekommen ist, was weder eingreift noch auftaucht, sondern immer wiederkommt, das ewige Plätschern der Wiederkehr."[46] Das Stillstehen, das aus der Affirmation hervorgeht, ist von der Dauer bestimmt und im Raum angesiedelt. Es kennzeichnet das Ornament als Zeichen ohne Referenz. +++ „Für das Zeichen als Form gibt es in der Tat keine Referenz. Das heißt: die Unterscheidung Bezeichnendes/Bezeichnetes kann man verwenden oder auch nicht. Es gibt nichts ‚Externes', was qua Referenz dazu zwänge; und es gibt auch kein Wahrheitskriterium für die Wahl der Ausgangsentscheidung."[47] Der Signifikant vertritt nicht das Signifikat sondern die Beziehung zwischen beiden hält den Spielraum zwischen Denotation und Konnotation offen. Dieser Spielraum ist Freiheitsraum. +++ Zuschreibungen/eineindeutige Beziehungen/Bedeutungen werden in diesem Freiheitsraum, der Grenzbereich ist, als Differenz obsolet. Die Unterschiedenheit befindet sich in einem andauernden Definierungsprozess. Dieser Aspekt des Ornaments

border crossings in both directions, it also allows expansion. +++ Ornament combines/embodies/visualizes itself as difference/distinction/separation and therefore detaches itself from any reference to an object. +++ To describe the ornament beyond its object relation and as the place of an activity, the concept of form—understood as a composition of individual elements—needs to be detached from the form itself. I then no longer conceive of ornament as a decorative element but as a process. This makes it necessary to redefine ornament and the ornamental concept. +++ I am going to use Niklas Luhmann's system theory as a guideline for this.[44] Based on his terminology, which he developed from a sociological perspective, I will try to verbalize my thoughts on ornamental creation.

Ornament as sign without reference

Initially, ornament has all the qualities of a sign. Based on semiotic theory that defines sign as something that refers to something else, one can state that an ornament accomplishes such a reference, even if this something else is nothing—in the latter case ornament, as a sign, visualizes and transports the very information that there is no information. I therefore call ornament a sign without reference since it does not reproduce a preset meaning and it does not represent something given. The philosopher Josef Simon once stated that a sign does not tell us anything about what it signifies. Ornament is neither semantic nor mimetic. It is not, in semiotic lingo, propositional[45] but immediate. It exists through structural relations as a marker, creating demarcations. It structures space without instilling meaning. Ornament is itself the place where ornamentation takes place and therefore attracts the attention of the beholder. +++ Like any other artistic creation, ornament communicates outside the everyday use of language. It communicates not through the use of concepts that require analytical understanding but immediately through the creation of an atmosphere that leads to aesthetic and symbolic comprehension through connotation. +++ Linear thought is indirect—preset norms lead to understanding within a stable frame of reference. I call this referential frame here the 'center.' Everything in the center is stable and hence standing still. Form and content are accepted as a unity, representation is unambiguous. This standstill, however, moves on a timeline and is a function of the development from beginning to end. With reference to immediacy, this standstill signifies affirmation. "The affirmation is the perpetuity of what admits neither of beginning nor of end. It is neither productive nor destructive but stagnant; it is that which has never come, what is neither staunched nor spurting forth but coming back—the eternal lapping of return."[46] The standstill that derives from affirmation is dependent on duration and places within a space. It characterizes ornament as sign without reference. +++ "There is indeed no referent for the sign as form; which is to say: one can either make use of the signifier/signified distinction or not. There is no 'external' point of reference that would force one to select either option; neither is there any truth criterion for choosing a first distinction as a starting point."[47] The signifier does not substitute the signified; instead, their relationship keeps the leeway between denotation and connotation open. This leeway is a free space. +++ Differentiations such as attributions/unambiguous relations/meanings become obsolete in this free space which is a border space. The

The conceptual starting point in my book work is the ambiguous formal principle inherent within the ornament. The self-referential development of the ornament's appearance is juxtaposed with a perpetual reflection of its qualities and function. Its self-referential dynamic questions the strictly formalized expression of any idea of progress, including its orientation towards purpose and goal. My aim—through the use of ornament—is to confront a linear concept of rationality with one that is multidimensional and symbolic. Its qualities are redundancy and variation. Ornamental play follows neither the rules of mimesis nor those of semantics.

Both ornament and text are signs and can be described as such. I understand ornament as a precisely formulated uncertainty that gains an objective character.

Ornament for me is a continuing iteration, an open understanding that does not allow for finite interpretation, that looks forward and back, that anticipates the future and keeps the past relevant. Its inherent recursive dynamic leads to "redundant information that includes information about things to come. The sign that follows then merely states more precisely and confirms, with limited information value, what had been expected." To accentuate their ambiguity, I try to keep the ornamental signs suspended between meaning and abstraction. The signs used for words and images have only a limited ability to refer to the role as substitutes.

The failure inherent in all representation, the gap that remains open in any sign, can be visually experienced in an ornament (as *Zierrat,* or decoration) and conceptually understood as a circular movement that endlessly circles the gap as the unreachable place. This gap is the door for that which can never be redeemed. From a positive angle, the gap is the driving force that makes us consider and reflect on its own presence and consequences, that stresses the simultaneous interplay of all senses and keeps the horizon of our understanding wide and open.

7. ENDNOTES

In the context of books, type itself can become the object of debate when the strict separation of the levels of form and content is abandoned. These two levels relate through their reciprocity as a momentum of content. The canon of traditional typography, i.e. the alternating relationship of text and image, is abandoned and can be questioned as a means of composition along the lines of the reciprocity of form and content. That includes the fact that signs are no longer arranged one-dimensionally along lines but rather open into space in multidimensional ways. Type as a medium of representation is limited in its form. The arrangement along lines in strings of letters is only one possible kind of typographic order. Visual or expressive typographies are an attempt at breaking up this order. (Onomatopoetic poetry tries something similar in the context of language.) Type and language are each tied to their quality as a medium and materialize through it. When *writing* is emphasized as a medium, type becomes an obvious element of form, a visual aspect of the book. They no longer disappear like transparencies and blend with their meaning (content). Thus the relationship between space and the signs imprinted in it is redefined. New centers of gravity are discovered and rhythmic shifts occur. These changes stem directly from the composition of the overall message of a book and must not be understood as a string of isolated messages or statements. The formal composition itself is expressive and conveys meaning. The achievement of formal effects is detached by the creative elements of a conceptual necessity. All these interventions take place in the pre-structured space of folded, turning pages—between two book covers.

When I stress type visually as the carrier of meaning, I am not only aiming at stylistic concerns but also at a formulation of content. For me, as an artist, the challenge is to deal with type not merely under the aspect of practical application but from a philosophical and semiotic perspective. Can philosophy influence visual appearance and vice versa? It seems to me that philosophical and semiotic considerations are absolutely indispensable in the context of this exploration. They serve as conceptual starting points for any reflection on the use of type as mediated language. They have an impact on the visual outcome of, for example, a book. From my point of view, they are the basis for any decision regarding composition and design when type is used artistically. If we look at art as an investigation into the perception of reality, we can also understand it as a reflection on the conditions and possibilities of type by aesthetic means. Visual expression and theoretical models guide and influence each other. They interact and both represent a possible approach to the expression of an idea.

To visually accentuate type as a carrier of meaning is, therefore, not merely a design effort but also a conceptual challenge insofar as type is understood as the representation of something that is not text. Such theoretical concepts cannot be derived from the craftsman's use of type but instead need to be developed out of philosophy and semiotics. Does philosophy influence the visual appearance or the other way round? I

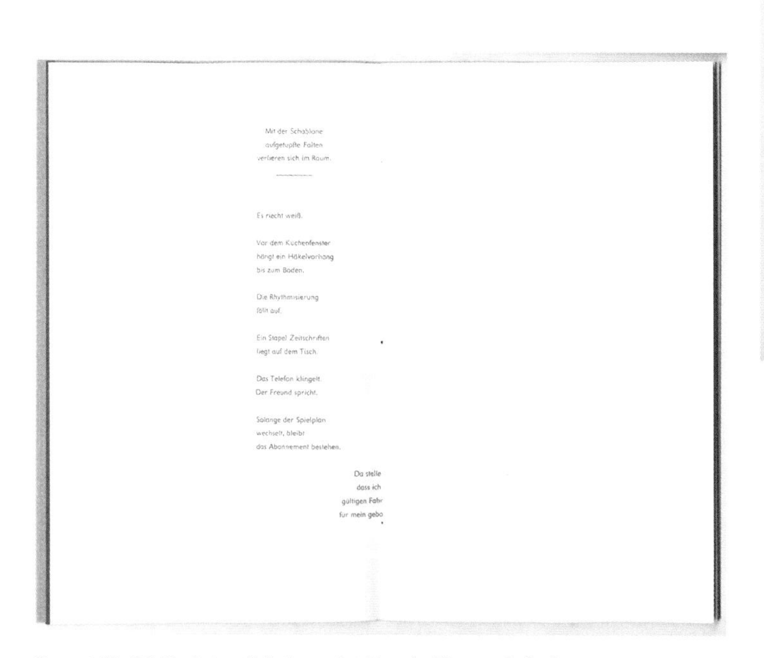
Mit der Schablone
aufgetupfte Falten
verlieren sich im Raum.

Es riecht weiß.

Vor dem Küchenfenster
hängt ein Häkelvorhang
bis zum Boden.

Die Rhythmisierung
fällt auf.

Ein Stapel Zeitschriften
liegt auf dem Tisch.

Das Telefon klingelt.
Der Freund spricht.

Solange der Spielplan
wechselt, bleibt
das Abonnement bestehen.

Da stelle
dass ich
gültigen Fahr
für mein gebo

Carnet 18, 2012, Anton Würth, artists' book. Photo: C.G. Boerner

Es tönt breit.

Aus dem Pappbecher
sickert Limonade
ins Gras.

Die Gleichmäßigkeit
ist spürbar.

Ein Holunderbaum
steht vor dem Haus.

Der Baum blüht.
Der Baum blüht nicht.

Sobald sich das Blatt
wendet, beginnt
der Kreislauf neu.

ich fest,
keinen
schein habe
rgtes Leben.

believe that the philosophical and semiotic perspectives are necessary. They form the starting point of any reflection on the use of type as mediated text and language. They do, in my opinion, influence the visual result and are the basis for any decision-making in the design of type and in the composition of the layout. At the same time, art—as a means of investigating the perception of reality—explores the potential of type. The visual results of the theoretical models interact and inform each other. They are alternative ways of approaching the possibility of expressing ideas.

My thoughts on type and typography inevitably lead to a reflection on the use of language. Language, type, writing, and spoken words are altogether different systems in the same universe. I cannot emphasize this *difference of the same* strongly enough. It is important to accurately perceive the deficiency of writing as the mediation of spoken language and to rediscover language itself as a medium of mediation. The gap that opens within difference itself and the deficiency of each system can become a driving force for artistic expression. *The critique of the modalities of typography as well as of the use of spoken language and the exposure of the taintedness of inner shifts is at the basis of the variety and complexity of artistic expression in the context of artists' books.*

Anton Würth, Berlin, May 2004. Revised and supplemented 2016; first published as a shortened version in *Artist's Book Yearbook 2006–2007* (Brighton: University of West England, 2005), 84–92. Translation by Johanna Bodenstab and Armin Kunz.

NOTES

1 Erich Rothacker, quoted in Jan Assman, *Das kulturelle Gedächtnis* (Munich: Verlag C.H. Beck, 1999), 66.
2 See Jan Assmann, *Das Kulturelle Gedächtnis*, 66.
3 "Scripting" is understood here as mere translation from the spoken language into written language. "Textualization" is the conscious use of writing, the intentional use of language as written text.
4 Marshall McLuhan, *The Gutenberg Galaxy* (Toronto: University of Toronto Press, 1962).
5 Ibid., 43.
6 For a detailed account see Michael Giesecke, *Der Buchdruck in der frühen Neuzeit* (Frankfurt am Main: Suhrkamp, 1998).
7 This is dealt with extensively by Marshall McLuhan in *The Gutenberg Galaxy*, passim.
8 Ibid., 105.

9 Plato, *Phaidros*, 275a, trans. Harold N. Fowler, (London: Heinemann, 1913)
10 Aristotle, *On Interpretation*, 16a, trans. E. M. Edghill in *The Basic Works of Aristotle*, ed. Richard McKeon (New York: Random House, 1941)
11 Horace, *Odes*, III.30.1.
12 On the relation between orality and literacy see Walter J. Ong, *Oralität und Literalität. Die Technologisierung des Wortes* (Opladen: Westdeutscher Verlag, 1987). Original: *Orality and literacy: The technologizing of the word* (London: Methuen & Co., 1982).
13 Aleida Assmann, *Erinnerungsräume* (Munich: Verlag C. H. Beck, 1999) 119.
14 Günter Grass, *Über das Zeichnen und Schreiben* (Göttingen, 1979)
15 Vilém Flusser, *Die Krise der Linearität* (Bern: Benteli, 1992), 19.
16 Felix Philipp Ingold, *Das Buch im Buch* (Berlin: Merve Verlag, 1988), 39.
17 Martin Heidegger, *Holzwege* (Frankfurt am Main: Vittorio Klostermann, 1980), 206.
18 Sybille Krämer, *Schriftbildlichkeit* in: *Bild – Schrift – Zahl* (Munich: Fink Wilhelm, 2003), 158.
19 Hartmut Günther and Otto Ludwig (eds.), *Schrift und Schriftlichkeit/Writing and its Use* (Berlin: De Gruyter Mouton, 1994), viii.
20 Ernst Doblhofer, *Die Entzifferung alter Schriften und Sprachen* (Stuttgart: Reclam, 1993), 13.
21 Oliver R. Scholz, *Bild, Darstellung, Zeichen* (Frankfurt am Main: Vittorio Klostermann, 2004), 112.
22 Krämer, *Schriftbildlichkeit* in *Bild – Schrift – Zahl*, 158.
23 Scholz, *Bild, Darstellung, Zeichen*, 124.
24 McLuhan, *Gutenberg Galaxy*, 50.
25 Ferdinand de Saussure, *Grundfragen der allgemeinen Sprachwissenschaft*, Berlin: De Gruyter, 1967), 29.
26 On the metaphysical dimension of the sign see Josef Simon, *Die Philosophie des Zeichens* (Berlin: De Gruyter, 1989).
27 This is different to a mere synthetic similarity; see Manfred Frank, *Was ist Neostrukturalismus* (Frankfurt am Main: Suhrkamp Verlag, 1984), 150; and Michel Foucault, *Die Ordnung der Dinge* (Frankfurt am Main: Suhrkamp Verlag, 1994), 101.
28 Stanley Morison, *First Principles of Typography* (Cambridge, 1950; first published 1930), 5.
29 Ibid.
30 Jacques Derrida, *Grammatologie* (Frankfurt am Main: Suhrkamp, 1994), 153.
31 Marshall McLuhan, *The Gutenberg Galaxy* (Toronto: University of Toronto Press, 1962), 54.
32 Ibid., 125.
33 Sybille Krämer, *Schriftbildlichkeit* in Krämer, Sybille and Bredekamp, Horst, eds., *Bild – Schrift – Zahl*, (Munich: Wilhelm Fink Verlag, 2003), 174.
34 Platon, *Phaidros*, 275A.
35 For a conceptual distinction between form and medium see Niklas Luhmann, *Die Kunst der Gesellschaft* (Frankfurt am Main: Suhrkamp, 1997,) 165ff. [*Art as a Social System*, trans. Eva M. Knodt (Stanford: Stanford University Press, 2000).]
36 Wolfgang Raible, *Von der Textgestalt zur Texttheorie*, in Krämer, Sybille and Koch, Peter, eds., *Schrift, Medien, Kognition*, (Tübingen: Stauffenburg Verlag, 1997), 29.

37 Hölderlin, letter to Schiller from September 4, 1795.

38 See: Anton Würth, *Röslein und Zierrat. Über das ornamentale Prinzip oder: das Ornament braucht keine Blümchen* (Offenbach: Klingspor-Museum Offenbach, 2012).

39 Maurice Blanchot, *Nietzsche und die fragmentarische Schrift* in W. Hamacher, ed., *Nietzsche aus Frankreich* (Berlin: Ullstein, 1986), 72.

40 Manfred Frank, *Was ist Neostrukturalismus?* (Frankfurt am Main: Suhrkamp Verlag, 1984), 482.

41 Niklas Luhman, *Zeichen als Form,* in Dirk Baecker, ed., *Probleme der Form* (Frankfurt am Main: Suhrkamp Verlag), 56.

*Herausforderung zum Wettkampf

Carnet 15, 2009, Anton Würth, artists' book.
Photo: C.G. Boerner

5156

5157 " [1]

[1] Johann Wolfgang von Goethe, Faust II; Erster Akt; Weitläufiger Saal; Rosenknospen, Ausforderung*; Vers 5144 bis 5157

Vorlageblatt, 2010, Anton Würth, artists' book. Photo: C.G. Boerner

XU BING

Square Word Calligraphy and *Book from the Ground*

BOOK FROM THE GROUND was written using various types of pictographs. One day in 2003, I noticed three small images on a pack of gum: *(please use your wrapper to dispose of the gum in a trash can)*. I realized that if icons alone can explain something simple, then they can also be used to narrate a longer story. From that point on, through various channels, I began to collect and organize pictograms from across the globe. I also began to research the symbols of expression employed by multiple professional fields. I worked on the book for many years. When I first harbored the idea, such a diverse range of symbols and emojis didn't yet exist. During those initial years, I witnessed the emergence of rich new content, which allowed me to complete the book.

After almost ten years of collecting materials, scrutinizing the concept, testing, revision, adjustment, and reworking, *Book from the Ground* has finally been published with an ISBN. The book's system of writing, in a certain sense, transcends current categories of knowledge and regional culture. It does not conform to any preexisting text-based knowledge. Instead, it conforms directly to the logic of daily life and of things themselves. Its legibility does not depend on the reader's level of education or degree of textbook knowledge, nor must it be acquired through traditional educational channels. Instead it relies on the degree to which the reader is immersed in the pictograms of contemporary life. Regardless of cultural background, spoken language or literacy, anyone with experience of contemporary life can read this book.

Square Word Calligraphy, 2000, Xu Bing, artists' books, red-line tracing book demonstration. Photo: Xu Bing Studio

Today, the trend toward globalization is making the world a smaller place, giving rise to the concepts of the "global village." However, this "big village" differs from the villages that first gave rise to individual written languages: the "villagers" now use a rich variety of spoken dialects and employ strange and mutually incomprehensible sets of symbols, while nevertheless living and working together. Current systems of writing face challenges that they have never faced before. Humanity's long-standing desire for a "universal script" has today become a pressing need. The significance of the Tower of Babel has only now truly begun to emerge. One can say that today represents a new era of pictographic script.

We had one principle in organizing the pictograms of *Book from the Ground*: to refrain from personal invention or fabrication. We were only to

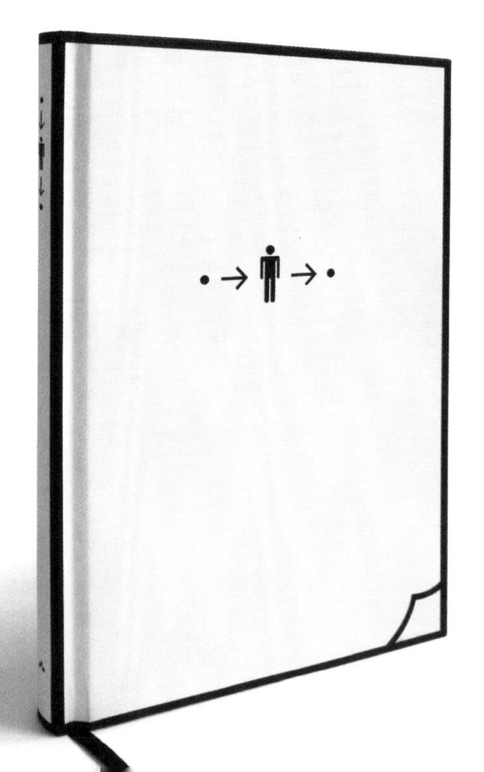

Above: from *Book from the Ground,* 2013, Xu Bing, artists' book, published by MIT and MassMoCA.
Left: *Book from the Ground* cover.
Facing: *Book from the Ground* installation (with interactive software), MoMA, NY, 2007.
All photos: Xu Bing Studio

A black man and a grey man sat next to each other in an airplane as it took off. The black man watched the grey man as he read from the airline safety card that had many, many symbols on it. The black man watched as the grey man read on and on,
and wondered what he was reading. The intercom announced, "Due to turbulence, passengers must return to their seats, fasten their safety belts, and may not get up to use the bathroom." He continued watching the grey man read.
He asked the grey man, "Hey, aren't you worried about the turbulence causing a crash? Don't be! I have flown a million times and the plane has never burst into flames or crashed into the ocean."
The grey man looked up from his book at his neighbor and said, "I'm not worried, and reading this safety card has given me an idea!"
The black man, seeming somewhat confused, asked "What idea?" The grey man handed him a pack of gum.
The black man responded, "Is my breath okay?"
The grey man said, "Your breath is fine. Look at the package." He pointed to the symbols on the pack of gum, but the black man was still confused. The grey man pointed to weather forecast symbols in a newspaper.
Then he pointed up to symbols in the airplane. . . He pointed to the symbol "very spicy" in a menu. . . He pointed to the symbols on a cell phone. . . He pointed to laundering instructions in a T-shirt. . .
He pointed to icons on an MP3 player, on a laptop, and so on. . .
#35
Then the intercom said, "United flight #35 is landing, fasten your safety belts and do not leave your seats to go the bathroom." The flight landed. The two men shook hands and parted.
The black man looked at the departure time on his airline ticket and then at his watch. He began running, only to slip and fall.
He saw the symbol on the warning sign and understood.

Above and facing: from *Book from the Ground*, 2016, Xu Bing, pop-up book. Photos: Xu Bing Studio

engage in the work of collection, organization, and formatting. Because they are already in use, these pictograms possess both a foundation of common recognition and the qualities of language. Most writing systems with the potential to spread become established through popular use and then take form through organization. Generally speaking, a system of symbols designed by an individual is a subjective result that lacks both a naturally formed logic and the basis for widespread recognition. The symbols do not support the characteristics essential for a system of writing: ease of mastery, commonality, and the ability to be reproduced. In *Book from the Ground*'s system of expression, all "characters" possess a source and an origin.

Above and facing: from *Square Word Calligraphy Copy Book*, 2000,
Xu Bing, artists' book. Photo: Xu Bing Studio

After its publication, *Book from the Ground* received positive feedback from the younger generation. This generation represents the super-territoriality and the future. Nevertheless, my sensitivity to pictographic symbols results from my tradition of pictographic writing and my cultural background of reading pictures.

More than twenty years ago I completed *Book from the Sky*, a book that nobody—myself included—could read. I created about four thousand pseudo-Chinese characters which conform to the linguistic rules of the Chinese character system. *Book from the Sky* is a paradox full of contradictions. People call its "texts" characters, but they cannot fulfill the essential function of "characters". People regard it as a "book," yet this "book" with the undeniable structure of a book does not in fact qualify as a book. Its external appearance and internal essence are at odds, allowing "hyper-realism" and "abstraction" to merge into one, solemn yet absurd.

Now I have made *Book from the Ground*, which can be read and understood by the speaker of any language. These two books, while completely different, do share one quality: regardless of what language you speak, regardless of whether you have received education, they treat every person in the world equally. *Book from the Sky* expresses my doubts and sense of alarm about existing forms of writing; whereas *Book from the Ground* expresses my view of an emerging trend in today's written communication and the ideal of a universal script. I know this ideal is a little too ambitious, but its significance rests in making the attempt.

Square Word Calligraphy interactive classroom installations, Xu Bing.
Above: 2002, Arthur M. Sackler Gallery, Washington D.C.
Facing top: Daryl Reich Rubenstein Gallery, Sidwell Friends School, Washington D.C.
Facing bottom: 1999, Third Asia-Pacific Triennial of Contemporary Art, Queensland Art Gallery, Brisbane, Australia.
All photos: Xu Bing Studio

Overleaf: *Book from the Sky*, 1991, Xu Bing, artists' books and scrolls; installation, Blanton Museum of Art, University of Texas at Austin, 2017. Photo: Xu Bing Studio

DEBORAH ULTAN

Counterculture Publications for Engaged Learning

I couldn't help but think why are these specific zines so important? They are unique and priceless, yet have no monetary value in our society. It goes against everything I am accustomed to in my day-to-day life.

Jesse Harris, student, Department of Communication Studies, University of Minnesota

TAKE AWAY THE "MAGA" from magazines and you have "zines", ephemeral publications that challenge publishing standards and distribution protocols of mainstream media. Zines are a form of literature that have a culture of their own, a culture that embodies active politically and/or socially charged constituencies involved in the promotion of print media that are, according to Marshall Weber "self-righteous, DIY, politically informed agitprop artist's publications."[1] A truly democratic medium, zines merge the personal and the political in formats that are typically low-tech, anti-consumerist, and uncensored; everyone who reads a zine can create one. Zines are often the result of innovative and aesthetic collaborations between artists and activists working to deviate from conventional agendas and mainstream press. While zines document daily lives and participation in social and political life, they likewise capture the cultural zeitgeist and specific historical moments. Alongside a deepening plunge into the cyber age and colliding freeways of social media and fake news, zine literature maintains a genuine, raw format that reaches communities in a way digital media cannot. Zines, writes Red Chidgey, "move between spaces where digital information loops might not reach and help create low-threshold opportunities for voice and representation within regulated, punitive, or otherwise inhospitable contexts."[2] Within the visionary context of zines,

All We Have Is Water, 2017, Monica Larson, Black Sister Press, letterpress print, 2017. Photo: Karen Carmody-McIntosh, University of Minnesota Libraries

they can leverage advocacy, speculation, and protest, and offer a direct way to react and give voice to issues of social justice, power, culture, politics, and the environment.

As the Arts and Architecture Librarian and Curator of the Francis V. Gorman Rare Art Book Collection at the University of Minnesota Libraries, I hold responsibility for acquiring general and rare research materials in art, architecture, and performance studies. The portfolio of these collections reflects my intention to focus on artistic activist literature and publishing. These alt-press materials serve as primary resources documenting the study of semiotics, cultural production and reception, political economy, and social justice. Zine librarians are leading the way in developing best practices for collecting, preserving, and cataloging this socially activist media of resistance and advocacy, despite the disruptive format and content of unconventional, radical publishing. Lifting the alternative small-press media materials out of the underground context from which they originally disseminate and into the academic environment supports immersive, exploratory study. Research in the arts and humanities that is laboratory-like, instead of passive and reliant on typical bibliographic hierarchy, can be effectively awakening and transformative for researchers, especially student researchers. The Marshall Weber Culture Wars Zine Collection, acquired for the Gorman Rare Art Book Collection, is a collection of posters, zines, comics, and mixed media that traces technological advances with image-making and rhetorical communication in the United States from the 1970s to the present. By way of this collection of personal and unmediated image and textual presentations, the zines and alt-press publications provide an unfiltered lens to history's social, political, and cultural movements. Weber states in his manifesto, "My primary motivation for collecting this miasma of paper was to document cultural and political dissent."[3]

Getting to Truths: An Exhibition Featuring Selections from the Marshall Weber Culture Wars Zine Collection was the first exhibit I organized, with the assistance of my colleagues Lindsay Keating and Shannon Klug, to introduce the newly acquired collection and its bold creativity and probing content. The exhibit revealed the raw aesthetics of the zines, which employ imagery, testimonial, satire, and storytelling in ways that explore, critique, question, and challenge issues without concern for censorship. We attempted to display as many zines as possible, creating curtains of them in clear folders hanging from the ceiling. Titles we displayed included *Earth First, The Coup, How to Measure Misunderstood Genius, Against Geology, Cats Against Cops, Gaylord Phoenix, Hard Times, High Performance*, and *World War 3*, which showcased innovative production methods and formats, from raw Xerox booklets to pamphlets, foldouts to printed and bound journals. The exhibit was

Zines and prints on feminism in the 2016 *Protest Publishing and Art* exhibition, Wilson Library, University of Minnesota, Minneapolis. With various artists including Lmnopi, Favriana Rodriguez, and Molly Crabapple (shown: prints from the Occuprint Portfolio, 2012). Photo: Karen Carmody-McIntosh, University of Minnesota Libraries

University of Minnesota Architecture and Landscape Architecture Library exhibition postcard for the *Getting to Truths* zine exhibition, 2014.

organized into genres that covered the most general and inclusive topics we identified in the collection: art, music, comics, poetry & fiction, hobo & travel, politics, feminism, environmentalism, humor, and intimate narrative. Illuminated within these categories were key socio-political topics and issues prominent in the 1970s and 1980s such as the Civil Rights movement, the global AIDS crisis and the Gay Rights movement, feminism and sexual liberation, the Vietnam War and anti-war protest, community activism, and the justice system. The historic zines, ranging from outrageous to subtle in their various combinations of imagery and text, expose decades of revolt against conformity and oppression. What's unexpected is how much these zines resonate with today's most pressing current issues.

Having caught the interest of the Gender, Women & Sexuality Studies department, Getting to Truths inspired one of the faculty to overhaul their class mid semester to include hands-on study of the activism, self-expression, and development of non-sexist media within the zine lit. Class discussions revolved around the impulse for zine-makers to integrate theoretical and political ideas with their own personal narratives and experiences and Adela Licona's ideas of "third space"—"Narratives deployed in zines offer everyday voices and counter-stories from third spaces and third-space subjectivities that can be instructive about and disruptive to dominant discourses."[4] Subsequently, the class visited the exhibit several times to study the zines, and then as a final project each student created their own zine. The zine-making project was a pedagogical tool that offered students the opportunity to connect their academic studies with personal experience and expression. The assignment invited students to consider their own objectives and topics and employ the raw, creative format to support their message. This encouraged a wholistic way of thinking about authorship, intention, and expression, and proved to be a meaningful, personal, and impressionable learning process. Indeed, neuroscience research on brain-based learning suggests that effective learning happens when the process involves making new and personal connections of the kind this assignment involved.[5]

I also partnered with several faculty members and structured class assignments around the Culture Wars collection and other protest and grassroots publishing that are in the Libraries' special collections. I

How Pictures Persuade: Zine Prompt, 2016, Elena Hristova, zine. Photo: Karen Carmody-McIntosh, University of Minnesota Libraries

designed zine research and zine-making assignments with faculty of two art courses and one communication studies course: *How Pictures Persuade (COMM 3645W); Digital Drawing (ARTS 3107);* and *Books, Comics and Zines (ARTS 3108).* Students in each of the classes were introduced to the zines and were then required to study the collection from a historic lens. They studied historical moments of visual culture in the United States with Occupy Wall Street and ACT UP posters, street murals, labor comic books from World War II, local comics, zines that embrace punk culture, gay culture, counterculture and feminist movements, and graphic novels. As one of the professors, Jenny Schmid, noted, "It is important to engage students as citizens—rather than as consumers—and zines have a rich history of anti-consumerism, political engagement, and community building."[6] Given ample opportunity to mine the zines for publishing techniques, content, and style, the students selected zines which they then researched and used as inspiration to create their own.

The students in the three classes were required to write reflections on their experience with the zines. Their assessments demonstrated how the informal and creative format of the zines distinctly captured their attention:

> I intended to just flip through it, but this happened to be in the graphic novel form, and I found myself sucked into the story and had read over half of it before I even realized. This magazine was of interest to me before I even opened it because I am aware that this country does not own its own bank, so I wondered where they were going to go and how the information was to be displayed.

> Hopefully zines can become a bigger presence among the younger generations, especially in this revolutionary time we live in.

Reflecting on the zine *FREE,* a student notes its persuasive presentation of the controversial issues with the justice system. In describing the content of the zine, the student reveals how the material engages and inspires critical thinking. Likewise, the personalized and colorful presentation of the zine triggers a response that is passionate and embeds the student's awareness and comprehension of the topic.

> My favorite zine was called *FREE.* The cover was a bright cherry red with a dark black crow seated at its base. It sparked my curiosity because it investigated a man who was wrongfully committed of

> murder. Leonard Peltier was a Native American activist who is serving a life sentence for the murder of an FBI officer. Brian Tripp had documented his court case and spoke out about his unfair trial. He made this particular zine to highlight Leonard's voice through handwritten notes from prison. The notes were heart-wrenching and very graphic of his guilt to the victim's family. Peltier was not pleading for his innocence but instead speaking up about the injustices done to his people. The zine was informational and persuasive.

Describing the zine *World Bank,* a student points out the effectiveness of the design, aesthetic, and the illustrative, storied approach. The student describes their visceral reaction to the content—the clash between economics and environmental issues—then takes their observations and fantasizes about authoring their own zine.

> The plays of light and shadow for the good vs. bad guys, and the way information is coldly received or imparted. The thing which inspired me most was two panels from the World Bank zine. The owner of the Bank, after being warned of potential environmental hazards for a specific population and area, in response to what previously sounded like helpful project plans, says to let him see. We get a small look through his glasses as he puts them back on in order to "see through his eyes" and we catch a glimpse of an entire forest on fire with the terrified/horrified face of an indigenous resident front and center of one lens. To this horrific view he replies that he sees nothing wrong, and the mass destruction in response to the project is described. That blew me away! It was such a powerful and complex message while still being fairly simple and straightforward. It got their point across, but allowed the readers to supplement in their own personal knowledge and experiences, which only strengthened the message. I hope to implement a few of the techniques and styles which I saw on display and read in the collection in order to clarify and strengthen my own zine. If my zine impacts anyone as much as my favorite zine hit me, I will be happy.

The students were instructed to research between two and four zines and were encouraged to be thorough about their research. They were given the incentive that their data could be adopted into the cataloging records and were made aware of how their contributions would enhance and support future discovery and access to the zines. To guide their research, they were given a template with a metadata schema derived from the Dublin Core Element Set, an accepted standard for the type of information/metadata that should be collected. The students quickly learned the challenges associated with researching non-mainstream media, works with unpredictable lifecycles, frequently changing titles or untitled works, and publications that lack designated authorship. In addition, they became alert to preservation issues as they handled the rare, fragile, and vulnerable material. Captivated by the zines, the students went out of their way to track down authors, pursue pseudonyms and artists, and to seek out these contacts for permission to possibly include proper or alternative names. Eventually, the Libraries' catalogers will take the additional student research for inclusion in the catalog records and the University of Minnesota Discovery catalog. This research assignment, with its deepened purpose and incentive to enhance access to the zines by contributing to the mechanism for searching them, noticeably raised the level of intent and participation of the students.

The final assignment for the two art classes and communication class challenged the students to create a zine of their own by applying the theoretical and practical lessons, goals and objectives of their particular course. Joining design and content, the students made zines that addressed topics on the environment, gender and sexuality, feminism, music, comics, politics, race, and a variety of personal narratives. The most successful student-made zines were included in the exhibit *Protest Publishing and Art: From the Copy Machine to the Internet*, which featured iconic publications illuminating the progression of radical print culture in the United States from the nineteenth century to the present. Posters, zines, comics, and mixed media in every technological form were carefully selected from the various Libraries' special collections to be displayed. Everything from Xerox to digital illustrations were selected to show an evolution of imagery and rhetorical communication. The student-made zines and the work of local artists who activate a message through visual and performance derivatives peppered the exhibit alongside the titles from the existing collections. A panel discussion with faculty, activists, and local artists, protest performances, and a printed brochure complemented the exhibit display cases.

The exhibit contextualized zines within an historical framework of radical print media. A nineteenth-century piece, for example, *Cartoons for the Cause*, with the illustration *The Worker's May Pole* by Walter Crane, was displayed alongside early twentieth-century labor publications opposing big business and capitalism. Several of the Industrial Workers

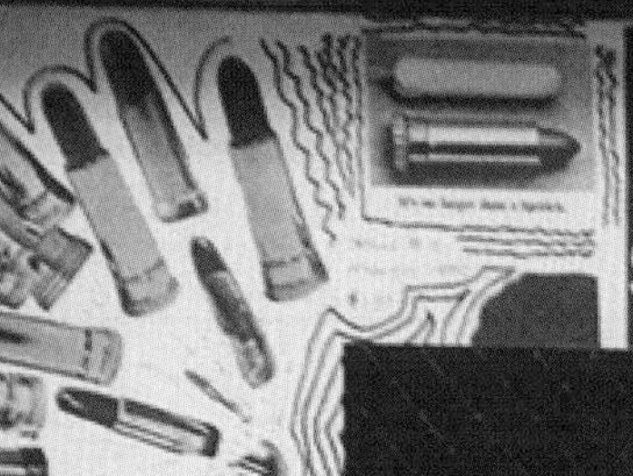

SHOTGUN SEAMSTRESS NUMBER 2

FIGURE 8

MOST REVOLUTIONARY THING YOU CAN DO IS LOVE YOUR

My Last Nerve

an XX zine for people who are Fed Up!!!

PROTEST

PUBLISHING

AND ART

COMING OUT

ISSUE NUMBER ONE
SUMMER, 2003

UNDERGROUND PRODUCTIONS 2004

ST PUBLICATIONS

the missing peace

truth and justice
in israel / palestine

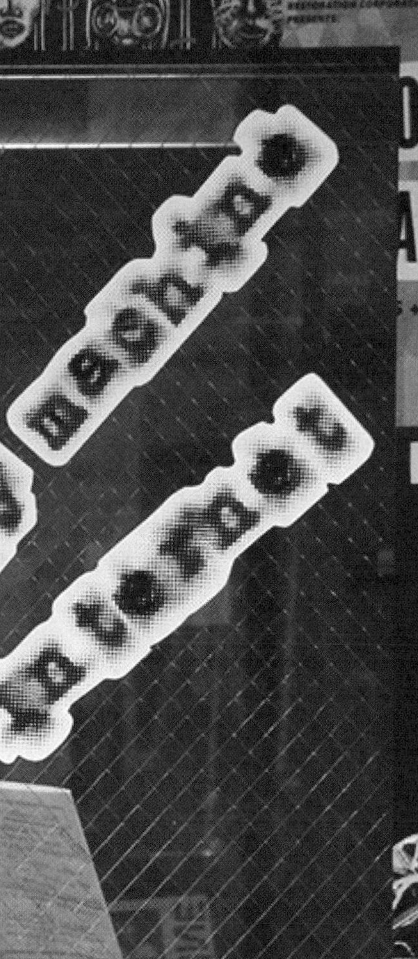
from the copy machine
to the internet
Guide to Water
BIG NOISE MAGAZINE INSIDE
ADBUSTERS
Culture
Jamming
BROKEN
HIPSTER
1980
HIGH

of the World (IWW) publications and pamphlets were exhibited alongside a local Minnesota publication from the 1980s that focused on human rights, diversity, and equal rights, *The Gathering Post: The Progressive Voice of the MN River Valley. Punk Rock Exposure* showed an unapologetically unrefined, unfiltered, politically charged "do whatever the f&*% you want" approach to the zine format, demonstrating how zine culture played an important role in dispersing information related to the confrontational music scene. An anonymous zine, *The Revolution Will not be Televised . . . But it will be on Twitter*, compares #BlackLivesMatter and #AllLivesMatter on Twitter, focusing on the social media platform as the location of radical revolutionary communication. Some of the student zines on exhibit were modeled after the "personal history" genre rooted in DIY culture and the 1990s Riot grrrl movement. Others, such as *Dakota Access Pipeline*, focused on specific political issues. *Wednesday Mourning* (2017) by Eric Isidoro reflected on mourning lost democracy the day after the Tuesday, November 7, 2017 election. Performing protest at the exhibit opening, a student paraded in a dress created by Marshall Weber (and part of the University of Minnesota Libraries collection) that features a quotation from Angela Davis, "The state thinks through our bodies." Artist student Reb Limerick and accompanying classmates performed in her designed and crafted protest garb *Air Flair*, *Fresh Air Frock*, and *Second Hand Smoking Jacket*. The panel discussion touched on three major themes relevant to zine culture, media, and protest. Summarizing the exhibit, the panelists spoke about the collaborative and individual approaches to zine-making and performance, sites and spaces of protest and messaging, and anonymous vs. conspicuous dissemination.

The exhibit *Protest Publishing and Art* assembled the research and work of students, faculty, local artists, and the community to think critically about zines, aesthetic form, and spaces of advocacy and protest. Students were enlightened to how artists, social activists, writers, and radical press historically merged advocacy, protest, and publishing. The library collections preserve, support, and provide opportunity to see and explore a historic view on radical print media. In an academic institution, a subject librarian curates collections to be diverse, historical, vital and relevant to the curricula, teaching, and learning. Their role in facilitating

Preceding page: View of *Protest Publishing and Art* exhibition, 2016, Wilson Library, University of Minnesota, Minneapolis. Photo: Karen Carmody-McIntosh, University of Minnesota Libraries

Thank You For Breathing the Air, 2017, Reb L. Limerick, performance, Wilson Library, University of Minnesota. Photo: Karen Carmody-McIntosh, University of Minnesota Libraries

the study and use of the collections is equally critical. The acquisition of non-traditional research materials, such as the Culture Wars Zine Collection, can serve to promote active, engaged learning and invites the students and researchers to collaborate with the library and collections as laboratory. The four classes, assignments, projects, and exhibits discussed here model the success of immersive study and the positive impact on students. The excerpts from student reflections evidence how their curiosity was awakened, how the raw, personal, quirky, visually, and conceptually compelling production of the zines resonated with them. With curiosity piqued, the students dove into the history and issues raised by the zinesters. The students demonstrated strong motivation and intention in their work, with the built-in possibility of their research being included in the University's catalog records and their handmade zines featured in an exhibition. Again, this tallies with the neuroscience research that suggests lessons involving immersive activities with potentially meaningful contributions to communities beyond the individual will result in deep engagement.

Once exhibited and made known on campus, the Culture Wars Zine Collection spawned interest. The collection has since become a valuable source for class study, research, and exhibitions. It models how primary documents, radical press, and non-traditional media resonate with students and invite intimate ways to study and understand cultural history, politics, gender studies, social justice, and environmental issues. Creative assignments and projects around the zine collection can foster immersive learning experiences that have impactful learning outcomes. Contact and interaction with the non-traditional, personal, and aesthetic format of the zines in the academic environment is effectively advancing the voice of diversity as well as cultural empathy and critical thinking about under-represented communities and socio-political issues.

NOTES

1 Marshall Weber, The Culture Wars Zine Collection Manifesto, 2010.
2 Red Chidgey, "Re-Imagining Zine Movements: Tenacious, a Prisoner-Made Zine, and the People of Color Zine Project" in *Media Fields Journal* no. 7 (2013): 8.
3 Weber, Culture Wars Manifesto.
4 Adela C. Licona, *Zines in Third Space: Radical Cooperative and Borderlands Rhetoric*. (New York: SUNY Press, 2012), 46.
5 See Ann Pace, "Brain-based learning for leaders: neuroscience continues to gain popularity as a scientifically sound approach to leadership development." *T+D* (Dec. 2012), 20.
6 Jenny Schmid, Associate Professor, Department of Art, University of Minnesota, 2017.

BIBLIOGRAPHY

Chidgey, Red. "Re-Imagining Zine Movements: *Tenacious*, a Prisoner-Made Zine, and the People of Color Zine Project," *Media Fields Journal* no. 7 (2013). http://mediafieldsjournal.squarespace.com/re-imagining-zine-movements/

Cure-Hendrickson, Noah, J. Harris, and M. Kimball, "Student Reflections," class assignment from How Pictures Persuade, taught by Elena Hristova, University of Minnesota, 2017.

Ganin, Netanell, Rhonda Kauffman, and Honor Moody. "Adventures in Mutual Metadata: Creating a Shared Zine Catalog," New England Technical Services Librarians, 2016. PPT Slides.

Grrrl Zines Network. http://www.grrrlzines.net/about.htm

Jeffreys, Jon. "The Libraries' Zine Collection: Inspiring Assignments and Art," *Continuum*. Minnesota: University of Minnesota Libraries, Spring 2017.

Licona, Adela C. *Zines in Third Space: Radical Cooperative and Borderlands Rhetoric*. New York: SUNY Press, 2012.

Moore, Anne Elizabeth. "Unofficial Histories: Zine and Ephemeral Print Archivists". *Punk Planet* no. 75 (September 2006). http://zinewiki.com/Unofficial_Histories:_Zine_and_Ephemeral_Print_Archivists

Ostertag, Bob. *People's Movements, People's Press: The Journalism of Social Justice Movements*. Boston: Beacon Press, 2006.

Pace, Ann. "Brain-based learning for leaders: neuroscience continues to gain popularity as a scientifically sound approach to leadership development." *T+D* (Dec. 2012): 20.

Weber, Marshall. The Culture Wars Zine Collection Manifesto, 2010.

Zoble, Elke. "Transnational networks of everyday feminist practices: from Grrrl Zine Network to Grassroots Feminism", *Labrys, Études Féministes*, January 2013. https://www.labrys.net.br/labrys23/culturepop/elke.htm

Zine Union Catalog Planning Project NEH HRCC Grant Application Project Description, 2014.

Gandhi ashram *jhola* artwork, c. 1960s/1970s, anonymous, Northern India.
Photo: Aaron Sinift

AARON SINIFT

Weaving Stories

Artists in Collaboration with Gandhi Ashrams

AT THE PRESENT CULTURAL MOMENT there is deep anxiety as to what can be known as objectively factual. In the digital world, lies are generated by design and instantaneously broadcast throughout the world via targeting algorithms. Digital information can be deleted from existence (or distorted) in a key-stroke from anywhere. At a time when we are challenged to clarify what is truthful and preserve what are facts, librarians and library collections have become indispensable in the material preservation and continuity of thought. As an artist who makes books, I feel that it is incumbent upon myself to create a work of art which preserves aspects of Truth, which materially embodies that Truth, which cannot be created digitally, and which engages directly with the world as an international social architecture of participants, including readers.

Since 1990 I have felt a longing for a world I experienced fleetingly, almost thirty years ago in India, a socialist economy in twilight—imperfect and moribund but refreshingly free of American-style consumer culture. What impressed itself upon my mind most clearly were the temporal qualities of art and life, how integral art is to the local community, and how it is supported by the local community. Season after season, for hundreds of years, enormous effort and creative energy is focused upon art forms which may only exist for a single festival night (if made of mud) or forever (if made of stone). Though these artists take pride in their work, they do not sign their names on it, and I found that the western understanding of "Art" and the artist's prerogative of self-expression did not apply to their self-perception. The 5 Year Plan project began from a desire to examine community-based art by engaging with Gandhi's living legacy in India through its ashrams. The project evolved into a *seva* (service) in honor of Gandhiji and a challenge to the accepted logic of neo-liberal capitalism in general.

THE IDEA

Returning home, to college, I used a homespun cloth Gandhi ashram *jhola* (sling bag) to carry books and whatever else I needed. The *jhola* had folk images on both side panels, one of national unity under the Indian flag, and the other a trio portrait of Indira Gandhi, Nehru, and Mahatma Gandhi, delightfully printed in three colors. Over the years I began to wonder about the artist who had done the drawings and reflected upon their anonymity. I recognized that the artworks were their *seva* to the Gandhi ashram and its ideals. I also began to notice that the homespun fabric, called *khadi*, seemed to get softer and more pleasant the more I used it. I wondered where it came from and what kind of society made it.

I remembered traveling in rural India and watching women threshing rice stalks against a rock to separate the grains. They were only twenty feet away, yet it felt to me as though we were separated by hundreds of years; I had the sensation of knowing that their existence on Earth was truer to the common baseline of humanity than my own detached modern western experience.

I dreamed of making a book out of *jhola* panels, a collection of Gandhi ashram artworks, and I applied for grants and scholarships to make it, but my pitch was too artsy for academic funding and too academic for art funding. I was washing dishes at home when an idea came to me that was asymmetrical and counter-intuitive but that seemed to incorporate all the elements that drew me to this obsession in the first place.

- It had to be Art.
- It had to be a form of service (*seva*).
- It had to cohere as much as possible with Gandhian ethics. It would be an experiment in Gandhian economics.
- It had to be independent and non-affiliated. DIY. No corporate sponsorship.
- It had to be "authorless" and by community subscription.
- It had to involve people and be of service to them, using what they do naturally, and making use of their excess abundant resources.
- It would draw on the fact that the artists I met were prolific and their nature was generous and compassionate. Gandhi ashrams spin and weave *khadi* cloth.
- To gain subscriber support, it had to reject altruism and create real value for them.
- To respect human dignity it had to reject any pretense of charity.
- To respect all participants, capital must not accumulate with one recipient.

- Half the artwork had to come from South Asian artists. Half the artists had to be women. There would be no more than four famous artists out of thirty total. All would be treated the same.
- If we consider "art" and "money" as energies (*shakti* or *"chi")* that are activated by human "desire", then these energies can be aligned to flow in a virtuous cycle of mutual service; therefore capital must be recirculated back into service in order to maintain the cycle. This would ideally have the effect of creating a community of interlocking abundances that would serve each other's needs.

To my knowledge, Doctors Without Borders (MSF) held the best record of service in international crisis relief. Could artists contribute their work to a collaboration with Gandhi ashrams in India to create a *khadi* cloth book to be sold to benefit Doctors Without Borders?

The book could be pre-sold as cheaply as possible to underwrite the whole run; then the book could be sold, with profits from the sales equal to the amount raised from selling advance copies of the book going to Doctors Without Borders. This seemed an audaciously delicious upending of the capitalist model.

It occurred to me how risky this project could be. Once started, failure to follow through would damage my reputation; if I created kitsch it would become an embarrassment, the world having enough crap in it already; if I lost or misused the subscriptions it would be dishonorable or fraudulent; and if it were ethically inconsistent, I ran the risk of dishonoring Gandhi's legacy and all who serve it. I spent months researching and thinking the plan through, and then months discussing the ethical implications with my wife and various friends, which I still do. I had lost my art-gallery job after the market crash of 2008 and was living in New York City on unemployment benefits, with only $0.01 in my savings account. To do this required careful planning and serious commitment. I had never been to a Gandhi ashram before, and I didn't know anyone who had. With all this in mind, I decide to call the project "5 Year Plan" for two reasons: 1. I knew most businesses make no profit for the first five years and 2. I could quit after five years.

THE FIRST BOOK: 5 YEAR PLAN

My wife had given me her old computer, so I began searching the Internet for information on Gandhi ashrams in India. This was difficult because in 2009 the ashrams did not have websites, and most still don't. I read graduate thesis and academic reports that had anything about Gandhi ashrams in them. I reached out to dozens of strangers and workshops, occasionally receiving replies but no solid information. I wrote to a wonderful friend in Vrindavan (Krishna's home town in India), Robyn Beeche. She immediately responded that she had just been to a textiles conference and that there was a real need for something like this, that weavers needed something they could make in large numbers, like a Gandhi cap, to support their families.

Eventually I reached out to a shop in New Delhi called People Tree, which had inspired me since 1993 with its activist books, handmade clothes, and an artist-freak sensibility which can seem very rare in India. I ordered research books through them and developed a rapport online with the owners. I explained what I was doing and why I was doing it and asked if they knew of any Gandhi ashrams I could work with. They gave me the phone number of Mr. Handa of the Gandhi Hindustani Sahitya Sabha (Gandhi Hindustani Literature Society or GHSS) in New Delhi. When I called him he was friendly, but the line was bad, and all I understood from our shouted conversation was that he was willing to meet me.

Once I had a few estimates from screenprinters as to anticipated expense and knew the rough cost of a meter of *khadi*, I thought through every foreseeable step and expense and made spreadsheets to anticipate quantities and pricing per book, asking for business advice wherever I could. There were still many unknowns, but it was feeling like it could possibly work. Several artists had responded to my invitation to participate; Donald Baechler was the first, then in May an email arrived from Yoko Ono's assistant: "This is a very interesting project, and Yoko would like to contribute her IMAGINE PEACE artwork."

About six months into my research, through a friend, I was referred to Tarun Devraj, a printer in Jaipur. This was a turning point, because he grasped the idea even better than I did and was willing to work with me. Tarun's questions made me realize how little I knew about what I was trying to do, but he caught the intention and saw its value. We spoke on the telephone only once for about a half hour, and it was clear to me that I had found the perfect collaborator. Months later, his wife, Nandita Devraj, told me regarding the project: "He said to me, 'finally, someone got it right'."

I decided to crowdfund the project through Kickstarter, which meant it needed a website. I had no computer skills but plenty of experience making old-school punk zines, so I designed the website the way I did my notebook pages, drawing in the links, writing all the text by hand, and pasting in the illustrations collage-style. These pages I scanned and sent

5 Year Plan book, 2010, Aaron Sinift et al., artists' book. The run was made using almost a mile of homespun handloom Gandhi ashram *khadi*.
Photo: Aaron Sinift

to Steven Warner, a long-time collaborator, who turned the drawings into functioning links. Friends of John Studer provided help with the sales page, and we launched the website on October 2, 2009, which by chance turned out to be Gandhi's birthday, an encouraging synchronicity.

Pre-selling a book is not easy, but I was helped by many friends in the art world, particularly Hudson at Feature Inc., whose contacts and endorsement went a long way and opened many doors for the 5 Year Plan.

Vijay Kumar Handa with teacher and young students, 2012, Gandhi Hindustani Sahitya Sabha, New Delhi. Photo: Aaron Sinift

I canvased constantly, following every lead that I had the energy for, sometimes wasting a lot of time but also learning what to avoid.

Everything taught me something: one apparently fruitless lead sent me to Booklyn Artists Alliance (now Booklyn), where I met directors Kurt Allerslev and Marshall Weber. Their vision was ahead of the curve on the possibilities of artists' books. They liked the idea and agreed to offer it to their institutional clients; it was enormously helpful in validating the project once The Boston Athenaeum and Stanford University pre-purchased copies for their special collections libraries.

In December I was stunned to receive an email written by Nandita Devraj, informing me that she and her husband Tarun had been in a car accident and that he had not survived. She would be carrying on our work together on the book.

By March 2009 I had raised $25,000 from pre-sales of the book and borrowed $15,000 to make the $40,000 necessary to create the edition of 180 books. I had my passport and visa to India and a few phone numbers and contacts but no real certainty as to whom I would be working with, never having met any of them in person. Everything would have to be worked out once I got there, and I only had three to four months to complete my work.

Arriving in India, my first stop was Varanasi, the city of Shiva, where I had studied sculpture and where I met with good friends who shared their advice. In Delhi I met Gurpreet Sidhu and Orijit Sen of the People Tree collective. They kindly offered me a place to stay as "artist-in-residence" in their workshop. This turned out to be enormously helpful because artists and activists were coming through constantly, offering advice and suggestions and unexpected perspectives while designers and cartoonists simultaneously worked out their ideas on various on-going projects. Their pace was purposeful yet relaxed, serious but casual, and for me very instructive and stimulating. Orijit pointed out to me that the 5 Year Plan logo, which I had lifted from an advertising label, was actually the symbol of Gemini Studios, the great 1950s Bollywood studio of Tamil Nadu—"A lift of a lift," he chuckled.

I then went to Jaipur to meet Tarun's wife Nandita Devraj at her company Rudraksh to see if we would be able to work together. I liked her immediately; her strength and fortitude did not obscure her sharp humor and insightfulness. Over the next four and a half months of working together we developed deep mutual respect and friendship. It felt strange to learn that Tarun and I had both been born within an hour of each other at the same latitude on opposite ends of the world on May 4, 1966. Strange too that this was reminiscent of the 5 Year Plan project logo, which depicts the Gemini twins standing together on the globe heralding the sun.

Once it was clear that Nandita would print and bind the book, it became necessary to find the appropriate *khadi*, approximately 1,400 meters of it. My next stop was meeting Mr. Handa.

The Gandhi Hindustani Sahitya Sabha is a pleasant two-story building next to the Gandhi Museum in New Delhi. It is set within a compound surrounded by a wall and gate next to a very busy thoroughfare. Inside is an oasis of calm; the school downstairs serves children from the community during the day, and in the evening it hosts theatrical rehearsals and music lessons. Mr. Handa and Mrs. Handa live upstairs, and that is where I met them, on a sunny afternoon with children running around. I felt at ease with them at once, and they showed me examples of *khadi* they had on hand, agreeing to take me to the ashrams that had produced them.

The next day we drove north of Delhi to Meerut, Modinagar, and Pilkhua to meet ashram workers and see what kinds of *khadi* they had available. These are very old institutions, dusty and quiet, like in a Pasolini film. In Meerut we spoke with a very stoic elderly man. I could see that he didn't quite understand why we were there so I showed him my sketches for the book, explaining that we wanted to honor Gandhi's *khadi* program. I saw he understood, and his eyes were slightly moist.

Today *khadi* is so forgotten and so undervalued in India that it no longer receives the respect it once had. Once *khadi* was seen as a proud living symbol of the Indian independence and self-sufficiency that Gandhi promised to the people, protecting the "soul of India (which) resides in its villages." The man I met, and many more *sarvodaya* ("universal uplift") workers like him, have served this dream since the 1960s and 1970s, despite government corruption and systematic de-funding. Now in India socialist institutions are being dismantled in favor of American-style "free-market" competition, which pits village *khadi* collectives against imported factory synthetics. Gandhi's dream of village self-sufficiency is being abandoned in favor of day-labor displacement into mega-slums. These ashram workers are the last holdouts of Gandhi's pastoralist vision.

We found the particular *khadi* we needed at the Manav Seva Sanidhi (People's Service Society) in Pilkhua, which Karan Singh, the founder, described as a "no profit/no loss service enterprise." I commissioned the homespun handloom cloth, 48 inches wide, to be woven for the book. It would take approximately two months to home-spin over 1,300,000 miles of yarn and then weave it into almost a mile of handloom *khadi* cloth of the type that Gandhi himself wore. I paid a deposit, and they agreed to ship the first batch in a few weeks to Nandita in Jaipur. In the meantime, it was my job to design and refine the book, compose the pages, edit the *5 Year Plan Literary Companion* book, and arrange or create color separations. Mr. Handa also insisted that I learn to spin cotton into thread, so I spent a fair amount of time at the ashram being schooled by the children there.

We printed each page as the *khadi* came from the ashram, slowly and steadily working through the 120-degree heat of Rajasthani summer, until finally in mid June I had done all I could and submitted all the necessary elements to Nandita for the final printing and binding. As a form of pilgrimage, I took off with my friends Janna Rose White and Jeremy Cheney to hike deep into the Himalayas up to the glacier source of the Ganges, where I bathed and gave thanks for the opportunity to realize this crazy dream.

Back in the United States, with eighty copies of the finished book, and another hundred to follow in the post, the work began to complete an edition signed by all one hundred artists. As they were spread over four different countries, we asked them to sign pieces of cloth and matched

Margoti Bhen, spinner, 2011, Manav Seva Sanidhi, Pilkhua, Uttar Pradesh, 2011. Photo: Aaron Sinift

them to their appropriate pages. We sent out sixty or so copies to the artists, helpers, and subscribers who had pre-purchased the book and promoted and sold the project. I gave myself ten copies and maintained myself with the proceeds so I could keep working. By the winter of 2011, 5 Year Plan had donated $5,000 to Doctors Without Borders. Later that year, Google NYC commissioned us to make 1000 *jholas*, and the following year we were invited to do another 1,500 Google NYC *jholas*. In total, both projects required 2,000 meters of homespun khadi, which created 1,800 days of work for spinners and another 200 days of employment for printers and tailors. 5 Year Plan made no profit at all.

THE JHOLA PROJECT AND THE SECOND BOOK: OTHER IMAGININGS

On February 2013 we launched the Jhola Project on Kickstarter. The idea was simple: for $20 we invited people to choose a Gandhi ashram *jhola*

Unknown weaver, 2011, Manav Seva Sanidhi, Pilkhua, Uttar Pradesh.
Photo: Aaron Sinift

printed with an artwork by one of fourteen selected artists, including Francesco Clemente, Yoko Ono, and Donald Baechler. The intention was to subvert art-world commodity value in the service of Gandhi ashram weaving collectives. People who purchased these *jholas* received extremely limited editions of woodblock-printed artworks by the artist of their choice for next to nothing, and in so doing created in total 400 days of employment. Five hundred *jholas* were made and delivered swiftly and all excess funds were donated directly to the ashram. At the same time, Boston University featured our work on the cover of their CFA magazine (Summer 2013) and commissioned a *jhola* specifically for the cover photo.

Our second book, *OTHER IMAGININGS*, started almost by chance encounter. I was in Varanasi and contacted a woman I had met before, Kahkashan Khan, a Gandhian activist who worked for World Literacy Canada as a coordinator and teacher. Kahkashan brought her new husband Jitendra Kumar, a charming man I instantly liked, and after a bit of reintroduction we jumped into a motor rickshaw for Sarnath to visit the Sri Gandhi Ashram. It was in a peaceful part of the village, surrounded by high white walls and composed of a series of low white buildings, a few trees, and a well. The gate was open, and people came and went. The occasional cow lay about the yard. Once there, I enquired about printed *jholas* and was shown a huge pile of rejected *jholas* from decades past. We went through each bundle and selected the best examples of each print we could find for the 5 Year Plan project archive.

In conversation with one of the ashram workers, we learned that the spinning and weaving happened there, but that the printing took place at the printing facility at the Sri Gandhi Ashram in Akbarpur, about 385 kilometers further north. To print about thirty meters of *khadi* cloth, in three- or four-color, making about 150 *jhola* panels, would cost approximately 7,200 rupees ($120). I had $300 left in my travel budget, so I suggested to Kahkashan and Jitendra that we print two ashram designs on thirty meters of *khadi* as an experiment. The remaining money would comfortably cover the travel expenses of them visiting Akbarpur, where they could take lots of pictures and then share their impressions with me. The information we got from the ashram was encouraging and it set me thinking about how we could make a book printed by a Gandhi ashram onto their own khadi homespun, as a work of art and artifact (art + fact), in which the medium personified the message.

Back in New Delhi I reached out to Mr. Handa with what I had learned, and he shared his vision for a second book, to be called *OTHER IMAGININGS* (inspired by Yoko Ono's *IMAGINE PEACE*). It would be block printed, smaller in scale, and should be funded by selling the only one single signed edition to an individual collector. Almost immediately I contacted Frank Williams, a patron of the first book whom I particularly liked and who I thought might enjoy the challenge of our untried experiment. He agreed, getting us started on a project which I told him would take about eighteen months, but would in the end take almost four years, due to developments at home and the birth of our son.

In February 2013 I knew that I would become a father and that I would not be back to India for at least a few years. I told Kahkashan and Jitendra that if this book were to happen it would be solely them in India working on the production, that we would provide all necessary funds and creative direction but they would have to make the individual decisions on the spot. The project paid for a Wi-Fi connection in their home, project expenses, and contributions to their family income, and I designed a profit-sharing plan for project participants. The whole thing was based on mutual trust and couldn't have happened otherwise, and I experienced a vertiginous thrill in taking a risk with a handful of strangers that would either result in a unique work of collective art or a humiliating dishonor.

Working with the Sri Gandhi Ashram in Akbarpur proved both richly rewarding and exasperatingly slow. Kahkashan and Jitendra visited Akbarpur and sent along lots of wonderful photos of their trip, which they seemed to enjoy. This ashram is part of Gandhi's living legacy, embodying a continuity of service for almost a century. They met the printing manager Gulabji and the screenprinting crew in their cavernous print workshop, explored the dyeing vats, and met the *dhobis* who must wash the *khadi* before it is printable. They had lunch in the ashram canteen, taking many pictures of the fire in the kitchen which Gandhiji ignited himself when he founded the ashram in 1920 and which has been kept burning ever since. To eat there, from this fire, was a kind of communion (*prasad*) for our friends.

The ashram has the dusty feel of a moribund institution isolated in time, sheltered by old walls while all around it the national culture has been largely overtaken by an ideology of American-style capitalism; ashram service is not seen as a future but as a throwback to the distant socialist past. In commissioning the *jhola* panels to be printed, Kahkashan and Jitendra discovered that the screens were made from hand tracings directly

Aaron Sinift and Kahkashan Khan purchasing old *jholas*, 2013, Sri Gandhi Ashram, Sarnath, Uttar Pradesh. Photo: Jitendra Kumar

from original artworks; this meant that the designs we wanted printed must first be handpainted in the proper size for the tracing. This had traditionally been the task of the ashram artist who had retired in 2004 but who lived nearby. Gulabji gave them the address of Jagdish Prasad Jaisawal, who agreed to do the painted copies but needed us to buy him paints and paper since he'd given them away years ago. The copies, made from two old *jholas*, were commissioned on the spot for 1,500 rupees ($25) each. Over the next two years we commissioned four more *jhola* art copies and six new works ($40 each) on themes such as technology, Khan Abdul Gaffar Khan, and one the artist instigated on his own about the Kargil War with Pakistan, which was to become part of the finished book.

Most of the workers are middle-aged or elderly men, and there are very few younger people to take their place when they can no longer work. The work is done slowly, without rush. In two years, we had had only twenty-two *jhola* designs printed, which was very frustrating for Jitendra (who did most of the Akbarpur work after Kahkashan too became pregnant). It took about a year before we found out that the workers were slow partly because they knew they would have to wait a long time for their wages, the institution being so cash-strapped. Our solution was to approach the ashram officials and offer to pay the workers directly, providing a donation to the ashram for use of their facilities. This worked very well and work sped up considerably, with bonuses being paid when our last page was printed.

Kahkashan gave birth to a boy named Kabir on March 22, 2014, and Jitendra was to be the "at-home" parent, very much bucking the trend in traditional Indian society. At the time I was also the "at-home" parent, taking care of a baby boy, Orion (born August 21, 2013), so it was decided that Jitendra would need to work on printing the *khadi* book closer to home. He located a Varanasi artist workshop called the Chinmoyee Kala Niketan, run by Snehashis Ganguly, and over the next two years we commissioned fourteen artworks to be printed as woodblocks onto homespun *khadi*. The block-cutter, Prakashji, cut forty-four separate blocks in his tiny shop. All the while, Jitendra was sending me photographs and little videos of our work progressing, and as fathers we shared baby news and encouragement.

Not only are Kahkashan and Jitendra breaking with parental gender norms in raising their child, they have also faced fierce societal rejection for their interreligious marriage. Jitendra is Hindu and from a small village of very modest means. He educated himself and went on to college; Kahkashan was raised by Muslim intellectuals who cultivated their daughter's strength, raising her on the campus of the Gandhian Institute of Studies from the age of five. The couple met while working for World

Printing crew at Sri Gandhi Ashram, Akbarpur, Uttar Pradesh, 2014. (Left to right) Kahkashan Khan, Ram Achal (color matching & printing), Lal Bachan (communications), Ram Charitra Verma (print supervisor), Gulab Chand Sharma (print division director), Mr. J.P. Jaiswal (ashram artist), Chauthi Ram (screen preparator). Photo: Jitendra Kumar

Literacy Canada. Their marriage has created deep friction with some family members and has the potential to incite violence from society at large. Even a "love marriage" is rare and against societal norms in India. Since the birth of their son, however, antagonisms are softening somewhat and there seems to be gradual reconciliation with their families.

Most of the workers who made the book – spinners, weavers, printers and block cutters – were paid between 120 and 300 rupees ($2–5) a day. To address the radical income inequality between ashram workers and myself in the United States, it was decided that copies of the book should be shared among participants so that the finished work of art would be of service to everyone. We allocated thirteen copies to Kahkashan and Jitendra. A copy was allocated to each artist, and to individuals who did much of the work, such as Prakashji the block cutter, and Arjun Paul the weaver, as well as to the institutions and ashrams that provided their services. If they preferred, we would sell their copy and give them the whole of the purchase price received. By the summer of 2018, we had paid out over $6,000 since completing the book in the fall of 2016.

IN SUM

Our 5 Year Plan project has created or supported at least 7,000 days of employment, mainly for those in the ashrams, most of whom are some of the world's most economically vulnerable people. Our *5 Year Plan* and *OTHER IMAGININGS* books are now held in at least forty institutional and private collections around the world, where they are a resource to students and scholars, and they are exhibited in the United States and India. Our profit-sharing and ongoing projects continue to provide supplemental income to activists and artists, even paying for the construction of a new home for one of the artists. The ashrams have benefited from the work our collaboration provides, but also from the fact that we honor their labor and sacrifice in a way that preserves their legacy. Copies of our books are now in the Gandhi ashram collections as part of their historical record, and for many Americans our books are the first substantive exposure to Gandhi's ideas, which inspire and sustain millions of activists around the world. I believe that our work helps to preserve an under-recognized facet of world history, a utopian vision shared by millions of people but which may be in its twilight. It would be truly tragic if we were to forget Gandhi's vision of sustainable self-sufficiency and be left only with the superficial popular perception of Gandhi as a simple "pacifist". Gandhi's vision was radical in recognizing early the dangers of industrial automation to village economies, and he acted upon a plan to restore economic balance throughout Indian society. Our artwork is your invitation to experience and participate in a great experiment in sustainable self-sufficiency, as envisioned by Gandhiji and embodied by those who love and serve their communities.

The process has taught me more than I could have imagined and introduced people into my life who have become part of an extended family. Together we are planning a third and final *5 Year Plan* book, to be grown from seed, that will address the realities of India's cotton farmers and follow the processes of spinning and weaving cotton all the way through to the completed *khadi*. We hope you will join us.

Above: Page from *5 Year Plan*, World Trade Center, 2010, from an anonymous Kolkata jute shopping bag, screenprint. From the collection of Prof. Andy Rotman, Smith College.

Left: *OTHER IMAGININGS,* 2016, made in collaboration with Kahkashan Khan and Jitendra Kumar, Vijay Kumar Handa, Nandita Devraj, and four Gandhian organizations in Uttar Pradesh. Photo: Aaron Sinift

Biographies

KURT ALLERSLEV is an experimentalist who explores the intricacies of the natural world as both artist and chemist.

Born in Chongqing, China in 1955, XU BING grew up in Beijing. During the Cultural Revolution he lived in rural northwestern China. In the 1980s, after moving back to Beijing, he received both an BFA and an MFA at the Central Academy of Fine Arts (CAFA). Since 1990 he has lived part-time in the United States, primarily in Brooklyn. He served as the Vice President of CAFA from 2008 to 2014 and is now a CAFA Professor of Graduate Studies. In 1999 he received a MacArthur Fellowship 'Genius Award'. He has also received the Fukuoka Asian Culture Prize and the Southern Graphics Council's lifetime achievement award in recognition of the fact that his "use of text, language and books has impacted the dialogue of the print and art worlds in significant ways." He is a Doctor of Humane Letters at Columbia University, a Cornell University A.D. White Professor-at-large, and was awarded the Department of State's Medal of Arts for his efforts to promote cultural understanding via his artworks. Among his hundreds of exhibitions are solo exhibitions at the New Museum of Contemporary Art, New York City; Joan Miro Foundation (Fundació Pilar i Joan Miró in Mallorca, Spain; ICA (Institute of Contemporary Art), London; National Gallery of Prague; the National Gallery of Beijing; the North Carolina Museum of Art; the Cherng Piin Gallery, Taiwan and the Arthur M. Sackler Gallery at the Smithsonian Institution in Washington, D.C.

A book artist and printmaker exploring the intersection of race, history, and perception, TIA BLASSINGAME holds a BA from Princeton University, an MA from the Corcoran School of the Arts and Design, and an MFA in Printmaking from Rhode Island School of Design. She has been an artist-in-residence at Yaddo and MacDowell Colony. Her artists' books can be found in library and museum collections around the world including the Library of Congress, Stanford University, and Tate Britain.

Blassingame teaches Book Arts at Scripps College and is the director of the Scripps College Press.

STEPHEN DUPONT is an Australian artist, curator, and photojournalist. He has received numerous awards and grants including the Robert Capa Gold Medal, the Overseas Press Club of America's 2015 Olivier Rebbot Award, the W. Eugene Smith Grant in Humanistic Photography, and the Gardner Fellowship at Harvard's Peabody Museum of Archaeology and Ethnology. His photography and artwork has been featured in far too many publications, exhibitions, and collections to list here. He is, in part, as his old hack photog friend Tim Page would say, an "anti-war photographer."

KAREN ELIOT is an art historian, critic, artist, and musician who is best known for their work with the Festival of Plagiarism, Art Strike, and other projects interrogating the concepts of authenticity, authorship, originality, and representation.

BRIDGET ELMER works as Coordinator and Instructor at the Ringling College Letterpress and Book Arts Center. She is co-founder of Impractical Labor in Service of the Speculative Arts (ILSSA) and founding member of Print St. Pete Community Letterpress. She received an MFA in Book Arts from the University of Alabama.

FLY-O is an illustrator, comics artist, painter, teacher, writer, musician, and, since 1985, a Lower East Side squatter, activist, and squat historian. She has been self-publishing zines and comics since the mid 1980s and her work has appeared in the *Village Voice*, *Juxtapoz*, *Punk Magazine*, *Maximumrocknroll*, *New York Press*, *The Comics Journal*, *San Francisco Bay Guardian*, and multiple other publications. Fly was the recipient of a 2013 Acker Award for "Excellence within the Avant-Garde" for her long-running PEOPs project, an ever-expanding collection of portraits and stories of extraordinary people who live life with passion and conviction.

GANZEER is a maker of Concept Pop, a kind of cultural insurgency that can be seen in his wide-ranging output, be it installations, prints, paintings, videos, objects, guerrilla actions in public space, writing, and also comix. Described as a "chameleon" by the *New York Times*, and recipient of the Global Thinker Award from Foreign Policy in 2016, he is now hard at work on an epic sci-fi graphic novel, *The Solar Grid*. His limited-edition screenprints and lithographs are sold through Booklyn.

SARAH KIRK HANLEY is an independent expert and critic in prints and multiples. She is a contributor to the journal *Art in Print* and a consulting expert for 1stdibs.com and Art Peritus Advisors and Appraisers, New York. Hanley holds an MA in Museum Education from the University of the Arts, Philadelphia, and a BFA in Printmaking and Fine Art from the University of Iowa, magna cum laude. She is a member of Phi Beta Kappa, ArtTable, and the Association of Print Scholars. She has held positions at Christie's, the Milwaukee Art Museum, and the Lower East Side Printshop.

RICHARD J. LEE is Booklyn's zine archivist and curator, and he puts on various zine-related events at Booklyn. He currently works at the Queens Public Library as a librarian. Before that he worked as the Queens Memory Project coordinator at the Queens Public Library, collecting oral histories throughout the borough. Richard's research focuses are small presses, radical American history, and zines created by POC.

FLORENCIA SAN MARTÍN is a PhD candidate in art history at Rutgers University, where she studies Latin American art and the history of photography. Her research has been supported by the Patricia and Phillip Frost Predoctoral Fellowship at the Smithsonian American Art Museum, the University and Louis Bevier Fellowships, Rutgers' Center for Cultural Analysis and the Chilean Formation of Advanced Human Capital Program. She holds an MFA from New York University's Department of Spanish and Portuguese Languages and Literatures (2012) and a BA from Catholic University of Chile (2006). Florencia is also an independent curator and the New York editor of Art Nexus.

MOBILE PRINT POWER (MPP) is a multi-generational collective based out of Immigrant Movement International (IMI) Corona, in Queens, NY. Members of the collective are from diverse backgrounds and bring a mixture of experiences to the table. They lead and facilitate weekly workshops and public projects to engage communities and explore social and cultural situations. For over four years they have been using portable silkscreen printmaking carts and methodology for participatory design in public spaces and collaborate with local organizations and collectives to engage communities in urgent issues such as brown-black solidarity, health equity, immigrant rights, displacement, educational injustice, cultural celebration, and creative problem-solving. All works, which are collaboratively produced, result in handmade books, prints, and/or public sculptures. MPP has published seven books, including *Message from Corona Plaza* and *Solidarity, Solidaridad*, and exhibited at museums, universities, and galleries, such as Columbia University, Queens Museum, and Interference Archive. The collective has created public projects throughout New York City, including regular projects in Corona Plaza, Queens. Members view their work as an ongoing process of creating and building solidarity and unity with the public, groups they collaborate with, and amongst themselves.

JANELLE REBEL is the Digital Curation and Special Collections Librarian at Ringling College of Art and Design. She has an MA in Visual and Critical Studies from the School of the Art Institute of Chicago. Her activities span critical graphic design, visual lectures, exhibition curation, and experimental bibliography.

AARON SINIFT (b. 1966) is an artist living in Beacon, NY. He has a BFA in Painting from the University of Iowa (1996) and an MFA in Painting from Boston University CFA (2000–2002). He started the 5 Year Plan project in 2009 to creatively collaborate with Gandhi ashrams in India as a Fluxus-inspired experiment in Gandhian economics. To date, *5 Year Plan* books are in over fifty private and Institutional Special Collections Libraries in the United States and Europe and have been exhibited at the Boston Athenæum; Feature Inc. in New York City; Studio 21 in Kolkata, India; The Printing Museum in Houston, TX; and the Central Academy of Fine Arts Museum in Beijing, China, among other venues.

SUZY TARABA is the Director of Special Collections & Archives at Wesleyan University, Middletown, CT, her alma mater. Over the past twenty years, she has shaped a diverse collection of artists' books with particular strengths in social issues and books inspired by earlier volumes. The Wesleyan artists' books collection is actively used in teaching across many disciplines.

DEBORAH K. ULTAN is the Arts, Architecture and Landscape Architecture Librarian at the University of Minnesota. Deborah oversees the collections for dance, theater, architecture, and landscape architecture, art, and art history. She writes and lectures on a wide variety of subjects including the digital arts and humanities, libraries, and visual and performance art. As a curator, she is the coordinator of on-site exhibitions throughout the University's libraries and campus and teaches courses on curatorial theory and practice. Deborah served on the Art Libraries Society of North America

Executive Board from 2006 to 2009, and remains an active member. She is currently serving on the board for the Minnesota Center for Book Arts.

MARSHALL WEBER has significant bodies of work in artists' books, collage, poetry, performance art, and video. He is co-founder and curator of Booklyn in New York City (since 1999), and was co-founder and curator of Artists' Television Access in San Francisco from 1984 till 1991. Weber has taught and lectured extensively and has curated hundreds of exhibitions globally. He is committed to supporting the work of activist artists and social justice organizations.

ANTON WÜRTH studied graphic design with emphasis on typography and book illustration at the University of Applied Arts in Augsburg and lithography at the Raffael Academy in Urbino, Italy. He has been working as a freelance artist since 1987 focusing on printmaking and book art. He lives in Offenbach, Germany, and regularly travels to Italy, the U.S., and Japan. Recent solo exhibitions of his work were held in Offenbach, Tübingen, New York, and South Bend, IN.

Sponsors

Jared Ash

Erik Delfino

Aaron Hughes
aarhughes@gmail.com
aarhughes.org

The Kelmscott Bookshop
34 W 25th St
Baltimore, MD 21218
info@kelmscottbookshop.com
kelmscottbookshop.com

Sharon J. Phillips, Attorney at Law
825 W End Ave, Suite 1E
New York, NY 10025
sharon@sjplegal.com
sjplegal.com

Ben Goretsky / 3DRetro
1851 Victory Blvd
Glendale, CA 91201
ben@3dretro.com
3dretro.com

Nicolas Lampert / Justseeds
justseeds.org
nicolaslampert.org

Deirdre E. Lawrence

Ruth Lingen

J. Pascoe
jpascoe.com

Mark Price / Twenty XX
markprice1026@gmail.com
twxx.us

Sandra L. Wamsley / Harvard Library
Cambridge, MA
library.harvard.edu

Beldan Sezen
info@beldansezen.com
beldansezen.com

Special Collections and University Archives, University of Vermont
538 Main St
Burlington, VT 05405
uvmsc@uvm.edu
specialcollections.uvm.edu

C. K. Wilde
christopherkwilde@gmail.com
currencycollage.com

Heidi Wilde
hwilde@wisc.edu

Patrons

Collins Memorial Library
1500 N. Warner St. #1021
Tacoma, WA 98416
libref@pugetsound.edu
pugetsound.edu/library

Bernie DeChant
berniedechant.com

Faulconer Gallery, Grinnell College
1108 Park St
Grinnell, IA 50112
grinnell.edu/faulconergallery

Interference Archive
314 7th St
Brooklyn, NY 11215
info@interferencearchive.org
interferencearchive.org

Susan Gosin / Dieu Donné
dieudonne.org

Soundtaxi
244 Madison Ave
New York, NY 10016
info@soundtaxi.com
soundtaxi.com

ARTISTS' BOOKS IN THE TWENTY-FIRST CENTURY